The Handbook of Animal Re

CW00552485

By Sarah Berrisford

Published by Pinchbeck Press

www.pinchbeckpress.com
email: taggart@reiki-evolution.co.uk

The 'animal reiki' kanji on the front cover was brushed for us by Eri Takase, Japanese Master calligrapher, who can be contacted at www.takase.com

ISBN 978-0-9563168-5-1

Contents

Introduction

My name is Sarah Berrisford, I am a Reiki Master Teacher, having trained through Reiki Evolution.

During this manual, I aim to take you through the different methods one can use to treat all kinds of different animals. The approach you may decide to take depending on the situation or the problem that you are hoping to aid.

This book is mainly aimed at those who have some experience with animals and have taken Reiki 1st Degree, however, I hope it can be an interesting and inspirational read to those who may not know very much about Reiki and would like to know more, or to encourage those who have experience with Reiki to take the next step and start sharing Reiki with animals.

What is Reiki?

Reiki is a Japanese technique; it aids relaxation and stress reduction, which promotes healing. Reiki is simple, natural and intuitive, bringing the body into a harmonious state, so that our energy is balanced. Balancing the bodies energy means that instead of just treating the symptoms, we aim to treat the body as a whole; spiritually, emotionally and physically. Reiki is not a religion; we do not need to follow a certain set of beliefs for it to work, however, Reiki practitioners do try to live by the precepts which Mikao Usui taught, these are simple ways to improve ones life, putting us on the right track.

The Reiki Precepts

The Reiki precepts are an important part of Reiki and life. Persons who practice Reiki try to live by the precepts, which are as follows:

The secret method of inviting happiness through many blessings…
Just for today,
Do not anger,
Do not worry,
Be humble,
Be honest in your dealings with people,
Be compassionate towards yourself and others.

By reciting the precepts whilst in the relaxed state of meditation we can help to train our bodies to live by them, just as athletes do and similar to self-hypnosis – we switch off the conscious, analysing part of our brain so that the subconscious part is just listening and able to take in and absorb the information.

Where does Reiki come from?

Reiki was founded by a man called Mikao Usui (1865-1926); originally the system was referred to as 'Method to Achieve Personal Perfection'. Mikao Usui's system was rooted in Tendai Buddhism and Shintoism. Tendai Buddhism (a form of mystical Buddhism) provided spiritual teachings, and Shintoism contributed methods of controlling and working with the energies. The system was based on living and practising the Mikao Usui's spiritual principles; that was the hub of the whole thing. Usui had a strong background in both kiko (energy cultivation) and a martial art with a strong Zen flavour (Yagyu Shinkage Ryu).

How can I learn Reiki?

Anyone can learn Reiki. I would recommend going to a Reiki Master Teacher whom you feel a connection with; look through lots of Reiki websites, read about the style of teaching, course information and support.

Reiki does not rely on ones belief for it to work; in fact people can still practice Reiki even if they have no belief in it whatsoever.

A Reiki course encompasses receiving an empowerment or attunement; this is your connection to the energy (chi). When practicing Reiki, one is channeling energy from an unlimited source instead of using personal energy.

Energy: the Animal to Human connection

Animals live energy. This is a simple statement which means more than one could probably explain, it is something one must feel.

All animals work with energy constantly; they have us 'summed up' in the moment we meet. We need no formal introduction – for animals it is an energy interaction. This is something that we too know how to do, but it seems many people have unlearnt how to read energy, something which is so natural, for example, if a person is sitting in a room feeling very angry, they don't need to say or do anything, we can pick up on the 'vibes' which tell us that person is angry. With practice at becoming more energetically aware we can pick up more about a person or animal, without communicating through sound. If people did this in relationships there would be a much greater understanding of each partner. Try this exercise with a close friend, family member, or partner:

1) Both persons sit down in a room next to each other, not too close though, let's not infringe on our subjects personal space.

2) Each person close their eyes, take a few deep breathes. Let your body become centered and relaxed.

3) Now just allow your attention to drift towards the person sitting next to you. Feel what your energy is doing, now that you have focused it on another person; do you still feel calm? Are you still taking nice even breathes? Does your chest feel relaxed?

4) Allow yourself to feel how the other person is feeling, allow yourself to connect energetically and receive a much deeper understanding.

This is also a good exercise to try when you are finding it hard to communicate with a family member; instead of trying to make small talk or ignoring what has become irritating to you, just sit down and allow yourself to connect energetically. The results can be quite amazing!

By practising our energetic reading and communication we can understand our animal friends so more easily. We use the same exercise as above, standing or sitting near to the animal and letting our attention lay on their energy. With practice, you will find that the relationship between animal and human becomes stronger, you may find that you can 'read' when something is wrong just by being around your animal and to go one step further, you may find that you know if something is wrong or bothering your animal even when you are not in their company.

The Animal Mirror

After a time of treating animals you may begin to notice that the animals you treat exhibit physical symptoms similar to their humans, you may also find that some problems within the animal are related to the owners emotional issues or what has happened in their life. When I first began to realise this, I thought "how terrible, the poor helpless animals, look at what the owner has done to them" - this is also the view of many healers. Along my path of treating and sharing energy with animals I began to realise that it is not always a case of the human 'passing off' their problems to the animal, but the animal being there for a reason to help their human and often the animal could not imagine why he would not share their owners load. This is illustrated in the story below.

Connection

Monty is a cheeky and confident part Welsh D, he and my sister Vicky are joined as a perfect partnership. Each year in Spring Vicky and Monty become affected

by the pollen, Vicky exhibiting the usual hay fever symptoms, whilst Monty develops a slight cough, watery eyes and feels a little down. As Spring approached I gave Monty a series of Reiki treatments with the intent of relieving any symptoms he would soon endure. During the third treatment, we were in a very deep connection, I focused on the symptoms with a deep intent that Monty need not 'pick up' Vicky's allergies, as the thought went out, I was immediately given the strongest feeling of 'why on earth wouldn't I help with my partners illnesses, this is part of our relationship and purpose, this is part of our connection and I wouldn't have it any other way'.

Course participants whom have met Monty on the Equine Reiki courses at Epona Equine Reiki centre will recognise the straight forward and to the point of Monty's attitude!

I feel it is very important to state here, that when we feel and see animals sharing their owners' issues, we should not be blaming people. Our animal guardians and friends have a purpose in life and we must trust in this connection that nature is taking its course. What would be the point of making the owner feel absolutely terrible that their animal is exhibiting symptoms because of them? Creating a mass of negative feeling and energy, which would completely undermine any Reiki treatment you have given. For healers who do feel the need to put blame on owners, it is simply their ego, coming forth to say "you're not doing it right, I'm better" this only coming from their own insecurities and problems. Often it is the suffering of a persons' animal which will bring them to seek out alternative treatments and ask about spiritual practices – there is a large percentage of students I have taught, whom have to come Reiki through their animals. Everyone has a path to follow, where ups and downs are stepping stones, the animal has come into the persons' life to aid with this development. Let us offer our support and guidance throughout a persons' learning curve.

As I meet your gaze and you look into my eyes,
You see deep into my soul,
The feeling of another being knowing my inner self,
Connecting through as one.
No outer appearances are perceived,
Just purely loved,
To feel so special from 'just' a look,
You know who I am,
What I am,

Why I am.

You see the purpose and perfection of the human soul,

You bring those qualities to the surface, just though being.

To be seen by you, is to truly see myself.

Energy check

Before we start a treatment we need to check our energy out put. Animals read our energy on the moment of meeting; they sense our emotion, whether we are nervous, excited, calm, happy, sad – the list goes on!

If we approach an animal with a nervous energy, they will wonder what you are afraid of; where is the threat? In a situation where we are feeling nervous about the treatment, it is important to take the following steps:

1) Breathe deeply and allow peaceful energy into your body
2) Don't go into the animals space
3) Stand back and connect to Reiki, then tell the animal that you are feeling nervous, you would like to share energy, but you are feeling nervous.
4) Allow yourself to really feel the nervous emotion.

By feeling the emotion we are able to accept how we are feeling, the problems with nerves are when we are trying to hide them, hidden nerves tend to make animals wary. If an animal is nervous or afraid of something he shows it. By being honest and open with the animal you will find that they would like to help.

Animals respond to love and happiness. A connection felt through love is one of the strongest available. When we feel true love whilst connecting, the heart feels bigger, the energy around the heart swells, feeling that you have the most beautiful light in your chest. Connecting though love is simple, we allow ourselves to think of our love for animals, not a needy love, the unconditional love whereby we would always do our best by our animals. The feeling you have when you look into your animals eyes. Animals recognise the universal energy of love; it is something they share freely.

Exercise – connecting through love

1) Make yourself comfortable
2) Connect to Reiki
3) Begin to think of all the love you have to give
4) Allow the feelings to build, you may feel a smile begin to emerge

When connecting through love, one will usually find that the animal connects to you first; they want to come in and share the love!

Become aware, learn to accept

Becoming aware of your being means that you can accept who and what you are, it brings calmness and peace, creating a space where you can enjoy the moment.

Letting go and accepting the animals past

It is only the thought process that makes something negative, not the actual situation, so you have the choice as to whether to let it be negative, whether or not you give energy to the negative or neutralize the energy. So, something terrible happens, your thought process can become more and more negative (which is actually the ego reveling in negativity) or you can choose to 'really feel' what has happened, feel it through every part of your body with no guilt, it has happened, there is nothing you can do about it, but only you can choose whether it affects you in this present moment. By feeling and becoming aware we accept the situation, this doesn't mean we have to like or be in favour of the situation, but we see it for what it is, it is life, it is experience, it is our learning in this world. In turn this allows you to deal with the situation that has happened.

The animals 'Trigger Response'

Animals live in the now, they are not thinking about what happened a few years ago. Although animals are in the present, only concerned with what is happening in the moment, obviously they do learn from their past, for example, say if a horse has had a bad experience and been beaten with a whip, this will create a trigger response, the trigger may be the whip, the person or the energy of the person; when confronted with one of these again, the horses trigger response is activated and he either goes into flight or fight mode.

We can help animals learn a new trigger response to the 'thing' they are worried about:

This meditation can be carried out in person or distantly

1) Make yourself comfortable and begin to relax.

2) Connect to Reiki

3) Picture the animal in your minds eye, allowing yourself to be open and feel unconditional love for the animal

4) Begin to send Reiki for a few minutes or until you find that you have a deep connection

5) Now, picture in your minds eye the circumstances where the animal is reacting negatively. You may be able to watch the scenes like a video clip in your minds eye.

6) Let any emotion that is coming from the animal be passed through, don't try to suppress any of the emotion, feel it with the animal and allow Reiki to flow, this may carry on for some time or it may only be 5 minutes – there is not a set time.

7) As you begin to feel the energy slow to a steady connection, begin to picture the animal in the same circumstances, this time you can picture the animal begin completely unaffected. You could visualize light or golden energy around the animal whilst he is in these situations. Keep the visualizations going so that you can see over and over again that the animal is being put in these circumstances yet he is completely unaffected; he is calm, happy and glowing.

Healing the emotion to heal the physical

Sometimes a physical issue comes forth due to an emotional problem. This is another reason why Reiki can be effective as a treatment. With Reiki we are treating the body as a whole, so instead of just treating the physical symptom, we are treating the underlying issue, bringing the body into balance so that it can heal itself.

Example

My cousins horse hurt himself in October last year. The Vet couldn't find out what was wrong with him and I asked Sarah what I could do to help him. I tried everything she said and read a lot on the internet and in Reiki books but as soon as I put my hands on "Nectar" I felt him very sad and unhappy. The reason for this was his owner had passed away, so abruptly taken from all of us and he was scared to go back to the place where he had been so many times with my dear cousin, and that was the "Feira da Golegã", this is a very well known fair where so many horse lovers go; from bullfighters, to horse breeders, they arrive from all over Portugal and Europe; they come to show their best horses.

I had 3 Reiki sessions with Nectar and guaranteed him his owner would always be there with him, and that we were all so proud of him and he was such a noble horse and he would know what he had to do.

The truth is the horse recovered fully, in less than 5 days to be at this fair, not even the vet could explain what had happened or how the horse went from completely not getting up and after 5 days being so tall and proud at the fair. I know why this happened, but to many people horses don't have feelings, they are wrong, they do have the same feelings, afraid of so many things just like we are and they just want to be loved, and they give us so much joy and love back that I can't describe.

Olivia Monteiro

Canine Reiki

Reiki can help dogs with many symptoms, physical and emotional. It is important to state in this section, that often the dogs that we treat that exhibit unwanted behaviour can also be solved through owner training. I would recommend anyone working with dogs and Reiki to watch 'Caesar Milan' – 'The Dog Whisperer', this program gives a greater understanding of how the owner affects their dog. A dog is a pack animal, the pack has a hierarchy, and it is important that the owner is the 'leader of the pack'.

We also need to look at how the dog is being kept, dogs need exercise, regular walking/running is vital for a healthy mind and body.

Through personal experience, I have found that sending Reiki to the dogs situation is just as needed as giving Reiki to the problem itself, for example, if we look at a vicious dog, we not only send Reiki with the intent to allow him to loose his aggressive tendencies, but also to his whole situation – this can lead to the owner having a better understanding and relationship with their dog and the means of this coming their way i.e. a good dog trainer may suddenly 'pop up' in their life.

Ways to approach the treatment

There are several ways in which we may approach a Canine Reiki treatment:

- On your lap
- Sitting at your feet or somewhere close to you
- Remotely
- Owner holding the dog or whilst in a cage
- Distantly

To start a Reiki treatment we also need to be aware of the dogs temperament i.e. whether he is friendly, anxious of people/surroundings, or aggressive. Are there certain times of day when the dog becomes excited or anxious, perhaps at dinner time or when he is expecting his walk; so it is helpful to ask the owner about the dogs routine, this way we can try to arrange his first Reiki treatment at a time when he can receive most benefit from it, being able to relax and enjoy sharing energy.

When possible I try to carry out treatments at the animals home, they are more relaxed at home and will tend to enjoy the energy for longer. Even if the problem the owner is having with their dog is due to him being agitated when away from home, still try to start with Reiki treatments in his familiar surroundings, after a few treatments we can then move on to using energy whilst in the situation which upsets him, by this time you have a bond with the dog, he trusts you and trusts the energy, he knows that you are there to help and you have already shown him in pictures through your minds eye how you expect him to behave from now on.

Sometimes the circumstances do not allow us to treat the dog in their home, in these cases simply trust in universe, trust in coincidences and trust in Reiki, you and he are there in that place for a reason, this is the time and place where the energy will be most effective and the universe has set the actions in motions to put the situation in the place which is suited.

Carrying out a treatment on your lap or with the dog close to you

Friendly dogs will often like to be as close to you as possible whilst receiving Reiki, obviously the size of the dog can determine whether you would like him to be laying on your lap!

- To begin, connect to Reiki, allow energy to filter from your body and spread to fill the room with beautiful bright light
- Begin to see light or feel energy coming from your hands, you may like to start stroking the dog, letting the energy be passed through to him as you stroke his back. Some dogs like to be stroked throughout the treatment.
- You may find that after a few minutes your hand(s) feels that it wants to stop in a certain area, if this is the case, let your intuition guide you and rest your hand on the area you have been guided to whilst sending Reiki.

- When you feel that enough energy has flowed into that area, you may find that the energy coming from your hands seems to slow or the dogs looks up at you to say move on, simply begin to stroke the dog again and allow your hand to stop where you feel.
- When the dog has received enough energy for that session, you may find one of the following
  - -the energy in your hands gradually stops,
  - - the dog gets up and moves away
  - - you have a sense that the treatment has finished

Some dogs may stay fast asleep after the treatment; bathing in the energy, in this case it can sometimes be hard to decide when the session should come to an end, if you have been sharing Reiki for over half an hour, the dog will have received a large amount of energy. Of course you don't have to worry about any animal over dosing on Reiki, they know how to use the energy and some would share energy with you all day, but to be practical one could say that a Canine Reiki treatment might last for 25-30 minutes.

Remote treatments

For canines which are timid or anxious, it is best to ignore them, pay them no attention and act as if you haven't noticed them.
- Sit comfortably away from the dog and don't look at him, preferably on the other side of the room
- Bring your attention to your heart, feel the energy of love in your heart chakra building, your unconditional love for animals,

perhaps think of your love for your own pet, keep focusing on your love of animals for around 5 minutes.

- Connect to Reiki, and feel the energy building around you, send the Reiki to yourself, to your animals, to your friends. By focusing the energy and your attention elsewhere, it shows the dog that you are not interested in him, you are completely unbothered by his presence and his reactions, which are of no consequence to you.

- The above actions have made you interesting to the dog, you may find that he comes closer to you, if he does just allow him to settle where he would like to, you may feel him connect into the energy you are flowing.

If the dog stays away from you this is fine too, he may prefer the energy from a distance.

Owner holding the dog or whilst in a cage

Sometimes it is necessary to have the owner hold their dog on a leash or for the dog to be caged whilst sharing Reiki. This may be due to the dog being aggressive, when dealing with canines which are likely to show aggression towards you please put yourself first, there is no point in putting yourself in a dangerous situation when a few precautions can be taken. Reiki works just as well from a distance.

When sharing Reiki with a dog whom is caged or on a leash, the following method can be used:

- Stand or sit at a safe distance away. If the owner is holding the dog make sure they have the dog under control, if he is leaping towards you, protecting his owner and pulling them it would be better for him to be caged, as this situation would be empowering the dogs frustration instead of calming him.

- Connect to Reiki, allow the energy to flow into your body and out through your hands.
- Fill the room with calm, loving energy, concentrate on what you are doing, keep your attention away from the dog, he does not have any effect on you.
- Once you feel a strong connection to the energy and have filled the room with Reiki, begin to send Reiki towards the dog, see the energy gently encasing him, calming his aura and softly seeping into his body.
- You may find that there is a particular place where you wish to focus the energy, just let your attention focus on this place – where thought goes, energy flows.
- If dealing with an aggressive dog, you may like to say silently to yourself "let my attention be guided to the area where the aggression is being held" and then send Reiki to this area.
- You may find that the dog has times of calmness and then starts showing aggression again, this is just part of the process of allowing the aggression to be released.
- Finish your treatment by sending Reiki to the dogs situation, send Reiki for the highest good of the situation.

Distantly

When you are called out to treat an animal it is a good idea to send some Distant Healing before the treatment. This way you already have begun the connection and the dog will often be more receptive when you arrive on the day.

The following instructions are a guide to send Distant Healing:
- Close your eyes and quiet your mind
- Connect to Reiki
- Begin to feel energy coming down through your crown, down the centre of your body and into your Tanden. Feel the energy build in your Tanden, spread through your body and flood the energy out of your body in all directions as far as infinity. Allow yourself to get into a nice easy rhythm.
- Say to yourself "I would like to connect and share Reiki with ………" (you don't need to have met the dog or know what he looks like, your intent will send the energy where it needs to go.
- Allow the energy to flow.
- Sending Distant Healing for around 10 minutes is a nice amount of time to establish a connection and begin the healing process. You may wish to send Distant Healing a few times before your meeting with the animal.

Canine Hand positions

Sometimes Reiki Practitioners feel more confident if they have hand positions to follow. This gives them a way of treating the whole animal, a base to start from and a process to follow. If a practitioner wishes to use hand positions but is unable to be close to the dog, they can simply use their intent to focus the energy on the area they wish to send it to. The following positions can be used if the practitioner wishes.

Position 1 - One hand on the chest. One hand on the back.

Through this position we connect to the heart chakra, sending love and healing. You can place your hand anywhere along the dogs back, just place it where it feels natural to put your hand.

Position 2 – One hand on the crown. One hand on the neck.
This position focuses on the throat and head, including the throat chakra, third eye chakra and crown chakra.

Position 3 – Hands on the shoulders

Allow the energy to spread throughout the chest and down the front legs, filling the body with Reiki.

Position 4 – Hands next to each other on the back, gradually move along. As you move along the dogs back, you can practice flooding energy or light down into the dogs body, filling his whole body. The chakras you are bringing to the optimum are the solar plexus, sacral chakra and root chakra.

Position 5 – Hand either side of the hind end
Allow energy to spread around the hind end of the dog and down into his back legs.

As you can see from the hand positions detailed above, one can treat the whole of the dog quite simply; hands on or remotely.

Below are a series of pictures showing a dog receiving Reiki:

To start we see Vicky holding her hands slightly away from Tracker, we can see Tracker stretch up enjoying the energy.

Tracker decides to lay on Vicky's lap. She feels drawn to hover her hands over his crown

Vicky moves on to the next position she is drawn to using; one hand on the chest the other at the base of the neck.

Tracker falls asleep – lovely and relaxed!

After ten minutes the treatment comes to a close. Tracker thanks Vicky.

A Schnauzer tale

As I walked in through the door, the phone was ringing, somehow the ringing sounded louder and more urgent than the usual tone. I hurried over and answered, a worried voice said; "Sarah, please can you send Molly some healing, she is in a lot of pain in her stomach, being sick plus diarrhoea, she is very ill and I don't know if she will make it through until the vet gets here". I immediately sat down and connected to Molly, in my minds eye I could see her laying down, her body tense and painful. As this picture came through, so did the overwhelming feeling from Molly; that she was going to die, the feeling was so strong and powerful that I disconnected for a couple of seconds, just to gather myself, so that there wasn't any worry or negative emotion being sent from myself back to Molly.

On reconnecting, I could see a swarm of panicked energy circling around the little dog; I surrounded her with a calming energy and watched as she accepted a vast amount of Reiki all over her body.

Just under ten minutes later, in my minds eye, I saw Molly get up and start walking around, looking happy. At that moment the phone rang again: "Sarah! Molly has made a miraculous recovery – she has just got up and is walking round completely fine!"

Left: Molly and her friend

A point to make about the above story is that when animals become ill, they can think that it is their time to go; instinct tells them that they are ill and will be caught by a predator, it is time for them to give up. So, just because we can feel what the animal is thinking, in this case, doesn't mean it is definitely going to happen.

Protecting mum

I was called out to see Bobby a beautiful Labrador cross, his owner was having problems in that recently, since her split from her partner, Bobby had started being over protective to anyone who came in to her house.

Bobby's owner was quite surprised that he didn't act aggressively towards me when I came in – although I was quite thankful and thought the Distant Reiki session the evening before had paid off a little!

I stayed in the room with Bobby and his owner left us alone, explaining that once someone was settled in the house he was back to his normal friendly self.

I connected to Reiki and immediately felt that there was a lot of responsibility on my shoulders. I became aware that Bobby was protecting his owner because this was what his owner was 'putting out', she no longer felt safe now that her husband had left and Bobby could see that she needed protecting; hence his behaviour.

I began to send Reiki with the intent that Bobby would no longer need to feel over protective, as I did this Bobby got up and walked over to me, he lay down next to me on the floor and as he did so, I could suddenly feel all of the Reiki going to his owner, there was such a lot of emotion and grief which needed to be let go off, so together Bobby and I spent an hour and a half connected together sending Reiki to his owner.

When the session had finished Bobby suddenly got up and barked happily, his owner came in, she said "I feel that you have been sending me healing, I have been crying for the last hour and a half, I didn't realise how much I had been bottling my feelings up, thinking I had to be strong and unaffected by recent events, thank you, I feel so much better!"

I went back to see Bobby and his owner on a weekly basis, his owner had decided that it was her that needed the Reiki treatments as after the first session Bobby had improved 100%. During each treatment Bobby would come and lay down next to the treatment table and join in with the Reiki session. A very special dog who had his own way of getting help for his beloved owner.

All for the love of a Spaniel

Helena was feeling ill, she was very dizzy and her whole body was aching. She lay down on the sofa, hoping a rest would help, however her body felt unsettled and she was very uncomfortable. Our black Cocker Spaniel, Tracker came and jumped up next to her on the sofa, he curled up and relaxed against her. Immediately Helena felt she could relax next to him, she wasn't as uncomfortable. After a few minutes she felt that she could let herself go into a restful state, she could feel his radiance joining with her energy and healing her body. After around 10 minutes, Helena was feeling a lot better; she suddenly got up and was able to carry on as usual, quite a turn around seen as before she had felt unable to move.

Our companion animals are important in our lives. They are here to help with our journey and will do so when we allow them too. They will also test us and give us problems to over come, teaching us about how we should react energy wise. We can learn vast amounts from our animal friends just by being in the now and observing how they act and enjoy life.

Amber the Bringer of War ... Reiki the Bringer of Peace!

Following a series of co-incidences (probably organised by the Universe) I found myself adopting a Samoyed dog. We already had three Samoyeds - Lexi (3), Kasper (11) and Jade (13) and had no thoughts about increasing the pack – until I met this old 'lady' at a Rescue Centre.

As it was my first Samoyed who set me off on my Reiki journey (when I was researching alternative methods of helping her fight cancer) I felt I owed it to her memory to offer this unfortunate dog a home. My only concern was that she would get on well with the current canines.
There was a very successful meeting in a big field at the Centre which involved lots of running about and very 'waggy' tails, so the official paperwork and checks were completed, and Amber came home. On the
journey I gave her hands-on Reiki, just in case she was not used to car travel ... and she went straight to sleep!

Amber (10) had had much of her coat (underneath, legs and tail) shaved off by the Centre staff as it had been too matted and tangled to groom. When I tried to groom her I understood why – she hated the brush and comb and snapped with no warning at whoever was daring to use them! It also became apparent that she was not really keen on having the other dogs around and tried to dominate my three by 'posturing' and biting them on the neck. She also seemed to cause my amicable trio to squabble with each other! She was very sweet with humans (as long as they didn't have a brush or comb) but very clingy and jealous when the other dogs came for a cuddle (which with Samoyeds is pretty much all the time). On top of that she barked, whined and scraped at the door as soon as she was left 'alone' downstairs – particularly at night - she obviously didn't count the two older dogs as 'company'. Quite a lot to sort out!

Of course, Reiki was sent daily with SHK to help her settle in. Her tolerance of being groomed improved and she behaved well on shared walks, but we still experienced very disturbed nights and she was also picking fights with the other dogs so had to be constantly watched.

After a week I decided to send Reiki not to Amber herself, but to the relationship between the four dogs. I sent the intention that they would all understand there was an abundance of food, water, shelter, space, exercise and love and there was therefore no need to compete for anything. What a difference! The very next day there was a marked improvement, with all four dogs playing together in the garden or just lazing about – and no 'trouble'. So far so good!

I now alternate between sending Reiki to Amber and sending Reiki to the relationships within the pack and things are improving every day - and the nights are very much quieter. She has been with us for just two weeks, and has made amazing progress thanks to Reiki – the Bringer of Peace!

After Reiki ... Lexi, Amber and Kasper.

Elinor Mary Thomas

The grieving dog

Ria had been sad and depressed, her owner called me to ask if I could help. Ria had lost her best friend 6 months ago and since this time had been like a different dog, not wanting to play, just laying in her basket.

During our first Reiki share, Ria came over to me and sat on my lap. After around 10 minutes I felt a huge emotional release, at this same time Ria let out a huge sigh and then shook her body. For the rest of the treatment she just stayed on my lap, gently dosing.

When I arrived for Ria's second treatment, her owner commented that Ria had actually seemed more lively since our initial meeting, they were very pleased and hoped that she would soon be back to her old self.

As Ria and I settled down for the treatment together my intuition told me to invite her owner to join us. We sat down next to each other with Ria in the middle. Reiki came flowing through very strongly, I could feel the emotion in the air around me, after around 10 minutes, Ria's owner burst into tears. We carried on with the connection and I began to feel peace descending into the house.

When the treatment came to an end Ria woke up full of energy, her owner smiled at me and said that she realised why I felt she had needed to join us.

Ria is now back to her old self, a playful, young at heart dog, always greeting her owner and welcoming people into their home.

The case study above shows how the animal to human connection is so important. Yes, Ria was upset about the loss of her friend, but she was unable to completely move on until her human had, because her human kept bringing up the fact that the dogs friend had died, bringing the death into the present moment, so in turn the dog was reliving the episode of losing her friend. Remember – it is better to have loved and lost than never to have loved at all.

Release your fears of the outcome

I have a very poorly whippet with an awful heart condition. I .am using Reiki and visualisation with him but this I do find hard as I want the outcome to be that he survives so much that I think I block the energy, although .maybe not as he is still with us.

Jenny Ward

Jenny's experience above is something most of us with a poorly pet can identify with. It is hard to release the outcome and allow energy to flow for whichever cause is needed. Your pet can still take Reiki and share energy with you, it is simply your mind is distracted by focusing so hard and wanting the outcome of living so much. Although hard to accept; what is going to happen, is going to happen and if you are having similar problems, I would suggest to sit and share Reiki, enjoy each others energy, think of the love and good times you have shared, no one can take these beautiful memories that your animal friends have given to you, they will be a part of you forever. We don't know how long any of us are staying here, so live for today, tomorrow might not happen yet!

A visit to the vets

A common issue animal owners encounter is when we have to make the dreaded visit to the vets. Our pets already know that they are going and become anxious, then we have to sit in the waiting room with even more anxious animals and their owners, and by the time we get into see the vet both the animal and ourselves can be a quivering wreck!

Below is a treatment outline for how we can try to overcome this issue:

1) Send Reiki to the situation, so send Reiki with the intent that everything is calm and easy, the car journey will go well – filling the car with beautiful golden light before you leave.

2) Send Reiki to the waiting room, visualize a lovely calm and peaceful energy, encompassing everything, so that any animal or person can feel the quiet and tranquility of the waiting room.

3) Send Reiki to the treatment room, again making it a nice place to be, thinking of clearing all the past negative energy away.

4) Send Reiki to your animal, visualize what is going to happen and that it is nothing to worry about, it is all for his own good, whatever the reason for his visit.

5) On the way to the vets and when you have arrived you may feel that it is easier to connect to Reiki as you have already put the energy there, so send as much Reiki and love to your pet as you desire.

Some responses to the above exercise:

- Owner could not believe that her dog was calm at the vets.

- Walking into the vets to find all the animals very quiet and calm.
- After doing the meditation, the vet rang up and said he was in the area and so would come out for a home visit.
- On arriving at the vets, everyone was very happy, the receptionist told me they were having a great day.

Frightful Fireworks

A question often asked of me is how to deal with the problems fireworks can bring to dogs and other animals. The story below shows how we approached this issue with Cassy.

Cassy was a happy dog, friendly and confident in herself, however, each year when the fireworks started, her owners could not console her, she would shake and hide underneath any object she could squeeze below, she would become very stressed, wetting herself. It seemed that each year, Cassy was reacting worse to the fireworks.

We started Cassy's Reiki treatments two weeks prior to the start of any fireworks, firstly I simply sat and offered her Reiki, after a short while Cassy came and sat next to me, she then proceeded to lay over my lap and fall fast asleep.

I gave Cassy three Reiki treatments which were all very similar to the first session.

On the fourth meeting I joined with Cassy, after a few minutes of sending Reiki, I began to picture fireworks night in my minds eye, I visualized the loud noises, flashing lights, and could straight away feel the anxiety rise in Cassy. I carried on picturing the effects of fireworks whilst sending Reiki to Cassy so that she would be unaffected, I pictured the fireworks banging, yet Cassy just hearing them as a dull background noise, picturing Cassy being calm and knowing that there was nothing to be afraid off.

I carried out the above visualization for the next three sessions, by which time Cassy was unreactive when I pictured the fireworks. At the end of the session I sent Reiki to Cassys' home, I visualized a Reiki bubble around her doggy blanket, so that she would feel safe and secure, for her whole house to feel calm, for her humans to feel relaxed and unworried.

As I looked out of the window at the first fireworks shooting into the air, I received a phone call from Cassys' owner, he could not believe that she was completely calm. Cassy remained stress free throughout the whole period, just laying on her blanket near her mums feet.

Left: My daughter, helping out with Reiki treatments.

Reiki for cats

Cats are intelligent and independent creatures, they know what they want and expect to it to be given. They understand that their human looks after them and cares for them, feeds them and is available for love when the cat has requested. Cats are self willed, they do what they want, when they want to.

Ways to approach the treatment

The felines personality and character dictates the way we approach the Reiki connection and treatment. As with all animals we let the cat decide how she would like the sharing of Reiki.

When treating your own cats it is often best to simply carry out meditations on yourself, allow your cat access to the room you are in and begin the meditation.

A suitable exercise is detailed below:

1) Allow yourself to become comfortable in your chair, feel your feet firmly connected to the floor. Take some deep breathed and let your body relax

2) Connect to Reiki.

3) Feel or visualize energy coming down through your crown at the top of your head, coming down through the centre of your body and into your Tanden.

4) Feel the energy build in your Tanden, and spread throughout your body.

5) As you exhale, flood energy out of your body in all directions, completely filling the room with a beautiful light energy.

You may like to listen to some relaxing music whilst carrying out the above exercise.

Carry out the above exercise each day, for say 5 days consecutively. You will most likely find that your cat comes to join with you and relaxes somewhere close to you.

Once your cat is coming in and deciding to join you for your Reiki sessions, you may decide to treat a particular area of your cat that is troubling her, simply by allowing your attention to focus on that point, or if your cat has decided to sit on your lap you may put your hands on the area which needs most healing.

When treating a clients or friends cat with Reiki, a similar approach is appropriate, however, I tend to send Distant Healing first, as this allows the animal to get a feel of sharing Reiki with a human before you physically meet. To send Distant Healing, you need only let your attention focus on the cat; your intent is enough to carry the energy to where it needs to go – where thought goes energy flows! Some people may have their own way of sending Distant Healing, which is fine too, the great thing about Reiki is that there are no set rules, it is simple and you can apply techniques that resonate well with you as a person.

When you arrive at your clients house to carry out the treatment, try to arrange your visit so that you are at a time of day when it is not feeding time, make sure there is access to fresh water for the animal and that you are feeling nice and relaxed.

Sit yourself in a room with the cat, she may deicide to come and see you straight away and Reiki may begin coming from your hands as you are gently stroking her, just allow the treatment to progress naturally from this, she may like you to carry on stroking her throughout the session or you may receive and inclining that your hands should become still and rest on a particular place of her body.

If your clients cat stays over the other side of the room when you are ready to begin the Reiki treatment, simply begin to carry out Reiki on yourself, just allow Reiki to flow into the room for say five to ten minutes. You may find that the cat connects with you and you may feel the energy being directed towards the animal. Let the energy flow for as long as the cat dictates.

Don't worry if you find it hard to know whether the animal has connected with you from a short distance, you could look to see if the cat is relaxed and falling asleep, which could be good indication that she has connected to you.

If it seems that the cat has not connected with the treatment, just send Reiki to a time that she wants to receive it. Remember animals choose whether or not they connect to the treatment, so there is not a force issue to worry about. Some cats will prefer to relax into the energy when they are alone, so again we are allowing the cat to decide when and how they would like to receive the energy.

Feline Hand positions

The hand positions which can be used on cats are the same as for a dog, again if you feel that your intuition tells you to put your hands in a different place, simply allow it to guide you. Treating with hand positions gives the practitioner a way of treating the whole animal, a base to start from and a process to follow. If a practitioner wishes to use hand positions but is unable to be close to the cat, they can simply use their intent to focus the energy on the area they wish to send it to. The following positions can be used if the practitioner wishes.

Position 1 - One hand on the chest. One hand on the back.
Through this position we connect to the heart chakra, sending love and healing. You can place your hand anywhere along the cats back, just place it where it feels natural to put your hand.

Position 2 – One hand on the crown. One hand on the neck.
This position focuses on the throat and head, including the throat chakra, third eye chakra and crown chakra.

Position 3 – Hands on the shoulders
Allow the energy to spread throughout the chest and down the front legs, filling the body with Reiki.

Position 4 – Hands next to each other on the back, gradually move along. As you move along the cats back, you can practice flooding energy or light down into the cats body, filling his whole body. The chakras you are bringing to the optimum are the solar plexus, sacral chakra and root chakra.

Position 5 – Hand either side of the hind end

Allow energy to spread around the hind end of the cat and down into his back legs.

As you can see from the hand positions detailed above, one can treat the whole of the cat quite simply; hands on or remotely.

Reiki to improve the relationship

Sugar and Spice had been rescued from a sanctuary, their new human had always owned cats and loved them very much.

I received a phone call regarding whether Reiki could help these two cats live together, the owner stated that they just would not get on, however, she didn't want to send either cat back to the sanctuary as she felt that she had a real bond with both cats.

I told the owner that I couldn't guarantee Reiki would help but that I would come and meet them and see how we get on.

Spice came straight to me, she couldn't wait to get in on the action and see what Reiki was all about. Sugar didn't join us for a while; she stood across the room looking with a disapproving sense toward Spice.

I began to use my intent to focus on sending Reiki to the cats relationship, I pictured the cats getting on well together, being happy and contented with each others company. At this time Sugar came to join us, she lay down near to Spice and I began to see their chakras, they seemed to join with energy so that their chakras were connected, we stayed in this place for around half an hour, until we all 'came back down to earth' at the same time. Both cats nuzzled me and the treatment had come to an end.

Sugar and Spices owner rang me the next day, both cats had made a complete turn around they were getting on!

The home wrecker

Tom was having trouble at home. Tom was a house cat but had begun to destroy the house when his owner left him alone. This was Toms' last chance; if he didn't begin to behave himself his owner was going to have to re-home him.

I connected to Reiki and felt Tom join with the energy. Tom stayed across the room, sitting looking at me inquisitively. I began to treat Tom's chakras, bringing each chakra to the optimum functioning. As I came to Tom's third eye chakra, I saw an image of his owner leaving the house, he was unsure where she was going and thought she wasn't coming back. We stayed sharing Reiki for a while until Tom came over and the energy slowed from my hands, I stroked him for a while and then we went to see his owner.

I felt it important to say to his owner that I had felt that he was unsure as to where she was going when she left the house. His owner decided that she would try telling him that she was going to work and would be back at 4pm.

A week later, Tom's owner rang me. Tom was no longer wrecking the house, she realised that when she told Tom that she was going to work and would be back at around 4pm he acknowledged her, not only that but she felt so close to him now, she felt that they had a stronger relationship and that she had a better understanding of him, as a very intelligent creature instead of just an animal.

Travelling tiger

Tiger had decided that he did not like his travel box. He scratched his owner whilst being put in and then would become stressed when closed in.

I sat down next to Tigers travel box and send beautiful light inside, I filled the box with a lovely inviting and calm energy. Tiger came over, interested in what I was doing.

I pictured Tiger asleep in his box, feeling warm, cosy and safe. Tiger nuzzled my hand and climbed on to my lap. I gently rested a hand on his back and he fell asleep.

After around 20 minutes I felt the energy slow and the treatment come to an end. I went to find Tiger's owner, who had kindly made me a nice cup of tea! As we talked about the treatment, Tiger's owner said that he was surprised that Tiger wasn't in the room with us as he was a very nosey cat and liked to be part of whatever was going on. We drank our tea and then went to find Tiger to say goodbye, we looked around the house but were unable to find him. Suddenly we both had an inclining 'look in the travel box' – and there he was, fast asleep!

The Shamanic Cat

I got my cats, Bea and Effie, from the local rescue centre. I live in a flat with no access to outside so I asked for cats that were suited for an indoor home, and said I would happily take older cats or ones with issues that made it hard for them to re-home (I am a sucker for an animal sob story). Bea and Effie were part of a group of nine cats kept locked up in a tiny room in upsetting conditions. They had never been outside so they could not be relocated to farmland as ferals, but they were so incredibly shy they couldn't really be handled either. I had to keep them in a pen when I first got them, but I knew with lots of healing they would do fine.

They are extraordinary creatures and, like all cats, they are very energy aware. The biting and scratching I was warned to expect never happened because, although they were very frightened animals, they soaked up the reiki and shamanic drumming and they quickly began to learn they were safe. Even before I could stroke them properly they would sneak on to my bed at night to sleep with me. At the time of writing I have had them only seven months and

they have transformed into two great little personalities.

Both of them are healers (as so many animals are!) but Effie's role in my shamanic healing work in particular has been extraordinary to see.

The smallest and most frightened of the two, Effie has revealed herself to be a shamanic cat! I am a shamanic practitioner and Effie loves the drumming and trance work integral to that. In shamanic healing we do work called soul retrieval, where we journey into non ordinary reality to retrieve the parts of a person's essence that has split off and been lost at times of trauma. We bring those parts back and reintegrate them into the body to create wholeness and wellness for the client. The first time I did a soul retrieval at home with the cats, I left the door open. I figured they wouldn't interrupt as they were far too nervous to come into a room with strangers.

My friend was drumming for me, my other friend lying down waiting for her returning soul parts. When I came back from my trance journey and sat up, the returned soul parts were around me waiting to be sealed into my friend's body. Most people wouldn't be able to see them, but cats can see spirit in a way we can't and to my surprise Effie came into the room and, looking around at them, meowed constantly. She sat herself down by my friend's head and watched me return the soul parts one by one, meowing to each as they went in. Once the process of sealing the energy body was complete, Effie gave a satisfied meow and walked away. We all felt that she had come to be a part of the most important aspect of the ceremony: welcoming the soul home.

If this was a one off, we could say that she was curious. It wasn't. Every time I do a soul retrieval, and most of the time I do similar work called power retrievals, she does the same thing. Even if I shut her out of the room, she sits outside the door and meows from the point that I return with the missing parts, and stops once I seal them into the body – even though she can't see what I am doing. My friends, students and clients all just accept this as a part of the process now, Effie has become part of the shamanic healing that I offer!

When the group of cats were taken to the rescue centre, Effie was taken to a 'foster home' of a volunteer instead because she had a little kitten. The rescue workers didn't want that kitten to be as scared of people as the adult cats were, and felt a proper home would be best to ensure he was regularly handled. Sadly the kitten died a few days later and she was returned to her family group straight afterwards, something which has left her needy and fearful of rejection. Despite still going through her own healing process, Effie seems to always want to be a part of the healing of others. I have always believed in a healing awareness in animals, but even I would never have expected that such a small and frightened creature would become such a healing force within a few short months. She is an exceptional shamanic cat.

Kay Gillard

www.starfirealchemy.co.uk

Reiki for Birds

All species of birds are sensitive to their surroundings, they require strong social interaction for emotional well being.

Many birds suffer with issues due to the stress of confinement and boredom, which leads to 'bad' behaviour. When we approach a bird to give Reiki we first need to have a grasp of understanding how it feels to be free, to be flying in the sky. Just because a bird has been bred in captivity doesn't mean that he doesn't know what that freedom feels like, the freedom of flying is instinctual to a bird. Once we have pondered on how it could feel to be so free, we may have a better understanding of how a bird feels in his cage – his instincts are telling him freedom, his life is telling him captive. We also need to accept that we can't do anything about his captivity; if we were free it would be unlikely that he would survive.

There are a few steps we can take when we treat birds, one is to recognise that any 'bad' behaviour he may be exhibiting could be down to frustration and boredom, we can encourage owners of birds who keep them in small cages to wither allow them flying time around the house or have a large aviary . Being able to fly can solve many problems we may encounter with birds.

Approaching the treatment

When we are treating captive birds with Reiki we need to follow our intuition as to how to treat. You may find that you receive the inclination to hold the bird, if this is the case, make sure there is not any sort of restriction; simply cup your hands around the bird without any pressure, so that if he wants to fly away he can do so.

The method I prefer to follow when sharing Reiki with birds is to sit in the aviary or a room in their house, so that they have enough space to go where they want to but you don't need to worry that they could fly away.

The following instructions are most suitable to treat captive birds:

1) Sit or stand comfortably
2) Connect to Reiki
3) Begin to fill the room with Reiki, you may like to visualize beautiful white light in the room.
4) Let your attention focus on the bird cage, and begin to flood the bird cage with white light, clearing away any negative energy that could be residing in or around the cage.
5) Let your attention focus on the bird, begin to send him Reiki.

6) Allow the treatment to carry on for as long as you feel the connection is there, the energy is flowing from your hands. Often bird Reiki treatments will last for say 15 – 20 minutes, but if the bird would like a longer or shorter treatment let him decide.

If you come to a case where a bird must stay in a small cage to receive his treatment, you can easily carry out the session remotely; you can follow the instructions above, filling his cage with Reiki and sending Reiki to the bird. Some practitioners like to place their hands on the cage during the treatment, whilst others prefer to sit back away from the cage. Neither way is better; simply follow your intuition as to what to do.

Be free – the teachings of an eagle

I waited with interest to watch the eagles flown at an animal park I was visiting. I watched with wonder as the eagle flew, soaring through the air, for a moment I imagined how amazing it is to be an eagle, feeling the air beneath my wings. As these thoughts passed through my mind I suddenly felt a great sadness, as the eagle came back to its handler. Knowing that actually this beautiful creatures true nature was to fly and be free and it was only conditioning which kept him trapped in a lesser domain, so to speak. Thinking of the eagle made me realise that his situation was the same as ours, as we are trapped by our own conditioning, although really just like the eagle, at any point we could fly free. We only need to realise that we are.

As the bird flies with wind beneath his wings,

I know there is a paradise waiting for our beings,

There is a freedom in this world, only some have realised,

No longer are they limited to the illusion of demise,

It is time now to awaken, to be who we can,

We only need accept, there are no limitations to man..

Bringing Reiki to the owner

I was asked to give a series of Reiki treatments to a bird who was self harming, pulling his feathers out. Ritchy was a tame bird, his owner was unsure as to why he had become agitated, his routine hadn't changed, he had regular time where he was allowed to fly around the house and his owner spent plenty of time with him each day, giving him attention.

I began the treatment by sitting in a chair with Ritchy free to fly around the room. I connected to Reiki and rested my arms on the sides of the chair with my palms facing upwards. To begin Ritchy was being quite vocal. I filled the room with Reiki and could feel a vast amount of energy flowing from my hands.

Ritchy flew over to the chair, he was standing next to my hand and began to touch my palm with his beak, although this could have been a little unsettling, as it would have been easy to receive a peck from Ritchy, something told me that he wasn't going to do this, he was just exploring the energy.

Ritchy flew away and came back a few times, each time he stayed a little longer, next to my hand. I could feel that he was enjoying the energy. Our session only lasted 20 minutes in total, I felt Ritchy disconnect, although he was still very friendly.

On my second visit to Ritchy, as soon as we connected to Reiki, he cam over and perched on the back of the chair, he stayed there, giving the occasional joyful chirp.

On the next visit Ritchy's owner told me that he had stopped hurting himself. His owner was very impressed with the effect that Reiki had and decided to learn how to channel Reiki.

Ritchy and his owner share Reiki on a regular basis and Ritchy has had no further problems with self harming

The Pretty Parrot

Whilst holidaying in Spain, I met a beautiful parrot, kept in a very small cage. I could feel an animals distress in the air before I could see the parrot and as I walked up to it I could feel Reiki flooding from the whole of my body. I stood near to the parrot letting the Reiki flow, I knew that there was little I could do to help the parrot in its situation, and this filled me with sadness, as I felt the sadness wash over me I had the intense feeling from the parrot that it was just happy that someone understood. Someone stopped by him and understood. Each day I passed the parrot, I would stop and allow Reiki to flow and we shared a special connection, I still send Reiki to the parrots situation, hoping that this will help him in his life, I trust in Reiki to help the parrot and know that he enjoyed just this simple connection with someone.

We can not always see the outcome that Reiki will produce but if we can trust that it will always work for the highest good, we can rest assured that what is meant to happen will happen.

Equine Reiki

On the one hand, horses are herd animals, they have one very simple

decision: to be weak or to be strong, to dominate or be dominated. There is no middle ground. However, if a herd of horses is examined closely, it will be noticed that two horses will have an especially friendly contact with one another. The horse seeks protection in the security of a large herd, but has a personal, trusting relationship with, usually, just one companion.

Interestingly, the lead stallion of the herd rarely has to use physical force in order to claim his position. It is the horses of lower rank who fight relatively harshly for their places in the lower levels of the hierarchy. Thus we look to lead the horse with the same methods that the non-fighting lead stallion uses, yet at the same time care and dote upon the horse a little in order to win his trust. A major problem that is occurring with equine owners today, is that they are constantly fighting with their horse for dominance and so they are more suited to the lower rank of the herd which will not provide the horse with a good wellbeing, physically or mentally.

Naturally horses live in open spaces and have the freedom to run wild. They are flight animals and so run from danger. Unfortunately, in this day and age, more and more horses are kept in circumstances that are far from their natural way of life. Equines which are stabled, in confined spaces, for long periods, can develop stable vices. These stem from being stressed, nervous and unhappy. Reiki is a really valuable tool for these horses. It releases their anxiety and can help many stable vices including weaving, box walking and wind sucking.

On approach to the horse, be calm and confident. Animals see us as energy, so if we approach them with scared or nervous energy, they read our energy and automatically think that there must be something to be scared or nervous about.

Creating your own space

Horses are very aware of their and your personal space. Imagine an energy field, approximately half a meter away from your body, if a horse steps into this energy field without you asking them to, then this horse thinks that they are dominant over you, this is not such a good thing.

Ways to approach the treatment

There are four main ways in which we share Reiki with horses:

- Giving Reiki whilst tied up or whilst the owner is holding the horse
- Giving Reiki free in the stable or small turnout area
- Remote Reiki – sending Reiki to the horse from a distance or over the stable door
- Distant Healing

Using Reiki on a horse tied up.

When we give Reiki to a horse which is tied up or being held by his owner it can make the treatment a little harder, as when the horse is free, he can maneuver himself to where he would like to be. It is important that when a horse is restrained we approach him and begin the treatment in a way that he would like and place our hands on areas which aren't sensitive or uncomfortable.

The hand positions I have set out below are not set in stone, but they are a good guide as to where one can put their hands on the horses in a safe manner and treat the whole of the horse. Some Reiki practitioners start treating the horse with one hand either side of the poll and the horses head over their shoulder – personally I do not feel that this is such a good idea, for the simple fact that you are putting yourself in a very vulnerable position. One could be pushed over by an unsettled horse or be head butted or worse still; knocked out if the horse moves his head quickly.

If you are asked to give Reiki to a horse that has to be tied up, the following simple procedure tends to be well accepted by all horses.

1) Enter the stable and make the horse back up, to give you plenty of space to open and close the stable door, without the horse coming to close to you or trying to come past you and get out of his stable. Next, put the horses head collar on and tie him up, using a quick release knot. Also make sure with the owner that the horse is used to being tied up and whether it has any strange habits whilst being tied up e.g. pulling back and snapping the rope, in which case you wouldn't want to be treating that particular horse tied up.

2) Step back away from the horse, so that you are completely out of his way if he moves around. Have a look at the safety aspect of things, if the horse does suddenly move around, are you going to get crushed against a wall? If the horse panics in the stable, have you got easy access to the stable door so that you can get out? These are things that you won't have to worry about with the majority of horses, however, there are some horses which are temperamental for one reason or another and you do need to look at safety for yourself.

3) Standing quietly away from the horse, connect to Reiki, feel the energy building within you, say to the horse by thought or out loud "take as much or as little energy as you would like"

4) Let the energy flow, feel yourself connect with the horse, feel as though there is a bubble surrounding you and the horse, anything outside of this bubble does not exist. All that is here is you, the horse and the connection of energy flowing between you. Stay in this position for between 10 and 30 minutes, until you see the horse relaxing, accepting

and enjoying the energy. Lowering his head, chewing, closing his eyes. Some horses may take a little longer to relax and may move around a bit at first; this is usually if they need to release something. Allow the horse to move how he wants to, so long as he isn't coming too close to you. If the horse is moving around and seeming a bit agitated; imagine him encased in an energy ball of calming energy that will let him release what he needs to. And remember to stay clam and confident within yourself; if the horse is having a release of some sort and is feeling anxious about this, he will look to your inner energy and if he sees that you are worried, this will make him even more worried.

5)   Once the horse is settled and standing calmly, you can approach him. The first hand position is to put one hand near the poll and one hand on the withers. If the horse is unhappy with one of your hands being near his poll, then put one hand either side of his withers.

Stay in each hand position for as long as you feel necessary, let your intuition tell you where to treat and how long for. As a guide; you may find that you are in each hand position for as little as 2 minutes or as long as 30 minutes.

As you move from one hand position to another you can scan over the horse to feel for any areas which are taking more energy. If at any point during the treatment the horse seems agitated or unsure about you focusing the energy in a particular place, you can return to standing away from the horse and send Reiki to that area from a distance. Horses are not all the same, some prefer to receive Reiki from a distance and others like the energy close to them. This can also change with each treatment, one session the horse may want Reiki from a distance and then the next session that same horse may want you to put your hands on him whilst channeling Reiki.

The horse will usually signal to you when he has had enough Reiki for that session, you will most likely feel that the horse has slowly stopped taking energy from your hands and you may have a feeling of the session being complete.

Below are a set of hand positions which I found most beneficial, when I first used Reiki on horses. The hand positions aren't set in stone, you will often find that you are drawn to a spot higher or lower, or that the horse moves himself to put your hands into the most beneficial position for him at that time.

These hand positions can be seen as a guide to follow if you are unsure where to start, you will find that as your confidence progresses your intuition will 'kick in' and you will find yourself wanting to place your hands in certain areas, simply listen to your intuition when this happens.

Position 1

Place one hand on the withers and the other hand on the poll. This

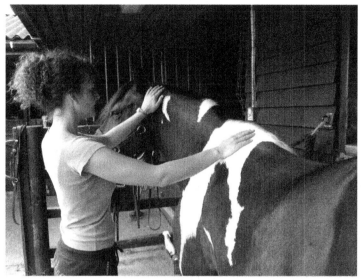

position usually relaxes the horse quickly. You will often find that you can feel the energy running down the neck from one hand to the other.

Some horses may not let you put your hand straight to the poll; instead, you are best to start of behind the horses' ear

Position 2

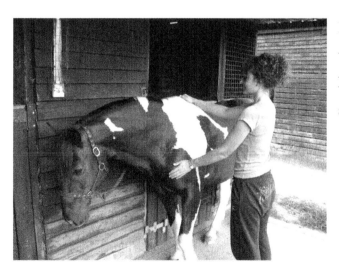

Place one hand on the withers and the other hand on the point of shoulder.

Position 3

Place one hand on the girth and the other hand on the chest to send Reiki to the heart.

Position 4

Place both hands on the horses back, dominant hand first with your non-dominant hand on top.

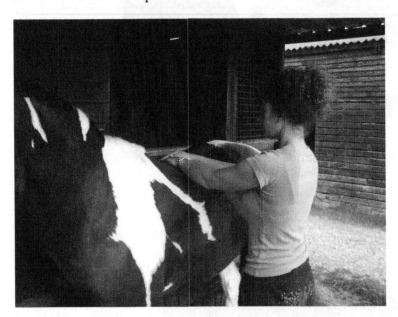

Position 5

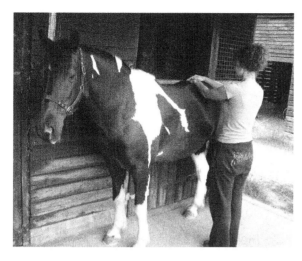

Place both hands on the loins.

Position 6

Place both hands on the croup.

Position 7

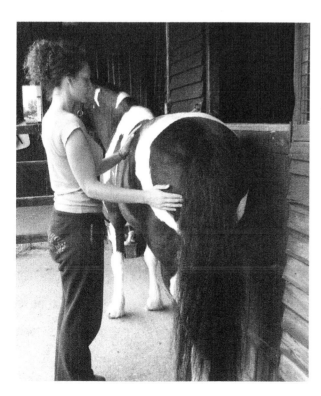

Place one hand on the point of hip, with the other hand on the buttock.

Position 8

Place one hand on the buttock and the other hand on the stifle. Some horses are sensitive or ticklish around the stifle area and so we tend not to actually touch them here, instead we hold the hand approx 10cms away so that we do not cause any aggravation to the horse.

Whilst carrying out these positions, you may want to try the 'many hands technique', so say for example you are in position 1, you can imagine extra arms on your body with the imaginary hands filling up the space on the neck between your left and right hands. Remember these extra hands are just as powerful as your real hands!

Intent

Reiki goes where you ask it and where it is needed. So if you are treating a particularly hot headed or maybe dangerous horse, you can carry out the session outside the stable. An upset or over excited horse can be calmed in a matter of minutes (or even seconds!) by sending Reiki from outside the stable.

We can also use our intent to send Reiki to a particular situation. For example, I send Reiki to our foals and their dams, with the intent of them having a trouble free separation. This seems to work very well and all of the foals and dams have been stress free when it has come to the time that they need to be separated. We can also apply this to a horse going to competition; sending Reiki to keep him calm and to apply himself fully on the day. In fact we can use our intent to send Reiki to any situation where we feel that it is needed.

Sending Reiki over the stable door: Remote treating

If you are asked to treat a horse that you are unsure about or has behavioral issues, for example, biting kicking or general disrespect for humans, then it is a good idea to treat this horse over the stable door.

You can either stand or sit comfortably in a chair. Make sure that where you are positioned is out of reaching distance from the horse. If he stretches his neck fully he shouldn't be able to touch you.

Connect to Reiki, feel the energy building within you; say to the horse by thought or out loud "take as much or as little energy as you would like".

Let the energy flow, feel the energy connecting you and the horse; you and the horse become one, at this moment nothing else exists, just you, the horse and the energy flowing between you.

When sending Reiki over the stable door you can use different methods depending on what you feel. Sometimes you may feel that just letting the energy flow and go where it is needed is appropriate for that session. Where as other times you may get the inclination that Reiki needs to go to a certain area on the horse and so you can direct the energy to this point using your intent.

If you feel it necessary you can still scan the horse; using imaginary hands;

1)   Close you eyes and in your minds eye see your hands hovering over the horse.

2)   Move the imaginary hands around the horse, start at the head, then down the neck, down the forelegs, along the back and body and finally down the hind legs.

3)   Take note of any change that you see or feel in the imaginary hands or in your own hands. This could include colour, vibrating, heat, coldness or the usual way in which you feel that Reiki is needed in a certain area whilst scanning.

When the horse has received as much energy as he would like for that session, you will gradually feel the energy flow slowing from your hands and then coming to a stop. This is the horses signal to you that he has taken enough energy. He may stay asleep, resting, or he may 'wake up' suddenly and come to the stable door.

Giving Reiki free in the stable

Leaving the horse free to move in a stable or turn out area is my preferred way to give a Reiki session.

Do not give the horse treats before the Reiki session as horses are very food orientated and if you do, many horses will spend most of the session trying to find more treats from you.

Firstly, stand in the stable or turn out area, close your eyes and put your hands into the prayer position, breathe deeply to still your mind.

- Affirm that the Reiki you are sending is for the highest good of the recipient and they only need take as much as they would like.
- Feel the energy flowing through your crown and down to your Tanden
- Feel the energy building in your Tanden

- See yourself connecting with the horse, see energy/ light surrounding you both, with your auras merging together. You both become one.
- Finally allow the energy to flow, feel it engulfing your surroundings, filling the area you are in and flowing to the horse.

You may have inclinations as to where to direct the energy, in this case, let it flow to these places. The horse may seem a little restless at first – perhaps he'll come over to you and sniff the energy coming from your hands and then perhaps stand over the other side of the stable. After a few minutes the horse will begin to relax. Signs of relaxing includes: chewing, licking lips, passing wind, lowering the head and deeper breathing.

Often the horse will come over to you and place his shoulders, for example, to receive Reiki. In this case use your intuition as to where to put your hands. After the horse has taken enough in that area he may then turn and place his hindquarters forward and so on.

The horse will usually tell you when he has had enough Reiki, if he stays asleep and you feel that you have completed the treatment, follow your instincts and finish. Often a horse that presents himself for treatment may come over and nudge your hands to say he's received enough for that session.

Don't worry if the circumstances above don't occur when you treat, every horse is different and each treatment to that horse will often be different as his needs for the Reiki change. So even if your horse just stands asleep in the corner of the stable, away from you, rest assured that Reiki is going where it needs.

Treatments generally last for around an hour, although they could range from 10 minutes for a first time of treating a horse to an hour and a half!

Reiki in stables/ horseboxes and other spaces

If a horse gets particularly upset by a situation, by being put in his stable for example, or loaded into a horse box, then we can use Reiki to create a good energy, atmosphere and feeling. To Reiki areas like a stable or horse box:

- Sit or stand comfortably.
- Connect to Reiki
- Feel the energy build in your Tanden
- As you breathe out flood the energy like bright light from your   body and fill the space around you

To Reiki tack or a particular object:
- Connect to Reiki
- Feel the energy build in your Tanden
- Let the energy flow and surround and engulf the object.

You can spend as little as 2 minutes doing this or as long as you would like or feel necessary. You will find that you know how long to carry on sending Reiki, so listen to your intuition and surround and engulf the object or place for however long you feel.

Reiki and Riding

Reiki before riding

You may hear some Reiki Practitioners say that you shouldn't give Reiki before riding. In one respect I agree with this as I wouldn't give a horse a full Reiki treatment before riding as it is good to leave the horse for at least a few hours after a full treatment to let him rest and allow him to use the energy for his best benefit. However, I do give Reiki to horses before riding, for example, before I ride my horses, I groom them first and then before I tack up; I scan over the horse, if I feel an area needs some Reiki, I will send energy to that area for around 5 minutes. When I scan the horse, I use my intent to let the energy know that I want it to focus on anywhere that will make the ride I am about to go on the best possible for the horse.

Reiki is also an excellent aid for horses that are highly strung and excitable when ridden. Just sending Reiki for 5 to 10 minutes before exercise with the intent of calming the horse during exercise makes a lot of difference. I have worked with many highly strung horses who show me again and again how valuable it is to use Reiki.

Instructions for sending Reiki before riding;

1) Connect to Reiki

2) Build the energy in your Tanden

3) Merge with the horse, see your auras merging together

4) Intend that the Reiki will go to the areas of the horse which will help him complete his exercise in the best possible way

5) Scan the horse

6) When you feel an area that needs Reiki, let the energy flow.

Giving the horse Reiki before you ride is very helpful for older horses who may suffer from stiffness for the first 5 to 10 minutes of riding; Reiki seems to loosen the horse before you get on, making it more comfortable for the horse and for you. Obviously though, if you do have a horse which suffers with stiffness problems, giving him full Reiki treatments everyday for 4 or 5 days will usually make a huge difference if not make the stiffness disappear completely.

Reiki whilst riding

We can send Reiki to horses and their riders whilst riding;

1) Connect to Reiki

2)	Place a ball of energy above the riders head and flood the energy down from the ball, over the rider and horse. You can leave the ball there to carry on giving Reiki even when you are gone.

This can help any horse and rider, from relaxing and calming a tense horse and rider, to giving more energy to a horse and rider who are looking more tired.

We can give Reiki to ourselves whilst riding, although I would advise to do this with your eyes open!

Instructions;

1)	Take a few long deep breathes and centre yourself
2)	Feel the energy coming down through your crown, down your body and into your Tanden
3)	As you pause before exhaling, feel the energy building in your Tanden
4)	As you breathe out flood the energy throughout the rest of your body and throughout the horses body

Carrying out this exercise for just a couple of minutes when you first begin your ride, can have a very positive effect on your ride, making it more enjoyable for you and your horse, so experiment and see what works best for you and your horse.

Reiki whilst riding for the nervous rider

There are a lot of nervous and unconfident riders that would really benefit from Reiki. It is very calming and can help both rider and horse, even confident riders can be a little nervous sometimes, for example, when they are in a new situation and are unsure of how the horse will react.

A helpful exercise for the nervous rider is as follows;

- Whilst walking around or as your nerves start to kick in, breathe deeply

- Pull energy down through your crown and into your Tanden

- Build the energy in your Tanden, feel the energy in your Tanden getting stronger

- Feel your Tanden and Solar Plexus area becoming stronger and stronger

- Let the energy flow out of your Tanden and Solar Plexus to infinity and beyond

- Keep this sequence going for around 5 to 10 minutes or sooner if your nerves have passed

Another good exercise for the nervous rider is as follows;

1) Whilst sitting on the horse, perhaps walking around, breathe deeply, take 5 – 10 long deep breathes

2) Begin to pull energy down through your crown, down your body and into your Tanden

3) Build the energy in your Tanden

4) Let the energy flow from your Tanden throughout your body, consciously feel the energy spreading up through your torso into your neck and head, feel the energy as it spreads to your shoulders and goes down your back, relaxing, calming and releasing tension in each of your muscles. The energy now carries on, goes down into your seat, down your legs to your knees and finally to your ankles and feet. Consciously feel the

energy as it spreads to each part of your body, relaxing each joint and muscle as it flows throughout your body.

Try repeating the exercise above 3 to 5 times to feel quite a difference, you will most likely find that your horse will also give you a better quality ride than usual after completing these exercises.

Reiki for performance

Reiki and visualization can really aid our performance with horses; whether you are entering a dressage test, competing in-hand, or jumping.

A suitable meditation to help with performance is as follows:
- The days before your performance is due, begin giving the Reiki treatments
- Let yourself relax and connect to the horse
- Begin to visualize what will be happening at the competition
- Show the horse the competition area In your minds eye.
- Begin to visualize the horse doing the performance, see him relaxed and listening, horse and rider as one together. If you are doing a dressage test imagine him going through the whole test, visualize how you would like him to look, how you would like the transitions to appear. If you are jumping visualize how you would like the horse to jump, see him clearing the jumps with ease, effortlessly clearing each jump, he confidently goes over each jump without hesitation.

The above meditation can be most helpful and effective for helping with performance, just completing it once, the day before the competition can have a very positive effect.

Horses reactions to Reiki

Most horses will show some of the following signs whilst receiving Reiki, these include:

- Lowering the head
- Licking lips
- Chewing
- Passing wind
- Producing droppings
- Going for a drink of water
- Relaxing a hind leg
- Closing the eyes

Some horses may even lie down and fall fast asleep. Don't worry if the horse you are treating doesn't show any signs, some horse, though not as many, will stay alert during the treatment, however, as soon as you leave the stable they may lie down and go to sleep, soaking all of the energy up you have shared.

I know what you're thinking!

It was a sad afternoon when my mum approached me to say that she may have to sell Zorro. Zorro is a Pure Spanish Horse, whom belongs to my mum, but I am his human. He is 11 years old and has been with since the age of 3. You see, due to the price of hay and straw escalating so highly, we were beginning to struggle with funding all of our horses, plus with building a new house the money would help to finish it.

The next morning, I was cleaning Zorro's paddock out, I began to think of the possible sale, telling myself that he would connect to another human and that we would be able to find him a home which he loved just as much as here.

As the thoughts passed through my mind, I heard Zorro gently neigh from the other side of the field, he came straight over to me, put his head over my shoulder and gave me the most meaningful cuddle. No words were needed, we just stood and hugged and knew that whatever would be would be.

A visit from the vet

I was asked to visit a friends yard whilst her horses injections were being done. She told me that her horses really disliked the vet. They were very suspicious of him and seemed to know when he was due as they wouldn't be caught.

When I arrived, the horses were in the field running in different directions. I asked my friend to take a step back, she was very tense, I explained that the horses would be feeling her tension and would think that there definitely was something *to worry about. She managed to calm her energy quite quickly and was very surprised when her horses both came over to her.*

We caught the horses and stabled them, I began to share Reiki with the horses, they both connected and I could feel an apprehension in the air. I pictured the vet coming and went through pictures in my mind, to tell them that he was coming to help them, the tetanus injection they would have would protect them from becoming ill.

The horses seemed to understand and calmed their energy to a normal level. I stayed with the horses whilst the vet came and neither reacted, the vet could not believe that these were the same two horses.

The example above shows how the different factors can play a part in a situation, number one, we have the fact that the horses had decided that they did not like the vet due to being mistreated and having to have lots of veterinary treatment in the past. Also we have the owner portraying to the horses that there is something to worry about, their owner was worried so there must be cause to be scared. By dealing with both issues we can allow a fast reaction to come through, I this case being completely relaxed around a vet.

Getting the pictures right

My lovely Saddlebred x Arab/TB mare 'Stardusr' was ready to start the breaking in process. She is a very willing mare and always watched whilst I was riding other horses, she wanted to be out there and joining in the fun.

Each time I started something new with Stardust, for example, putting the bridle on, I explained to her that this was to get her ready for being ridden, I would then picture us riding together, cantering along the grass tracks, with the feeling of fun and enjoyment.

I began to notice that when I had finished each training session with Stardust she wasn't happy, she was fine whilst doing the training, couldn't have been happier and more cooperative. The problem was when I had finished and put her out in her field. As I took her head collar off she would lay her ears back and look at me with a grumpy face. This was not like Stardust at all, although she is a lead mare and very clever, she is always friendly.

Whilst talking to a friend on the phone, I told her about Stardust, as I was telling the story a light bulb seemed to switch on – Stardust was getting annoyed because she wanted to be ridden, each time we did some training, I had been showing her being ridden in pictures.

The next time I bought Stardust into the arena, I decided I should get on her, I stood next to her and pictured what I would do, she looked at me and sighed at me, as if to say "well you've taken your time, I've been waiting for ages". Stardust was brilliant, completely unphased and relaxed. Needless to say, when I put Stardust out in her paddock she no longer laid her ears back; instead she stayed for a stroke and a scratch.

The fence breaker

Cloud had decided to become an escape artist, taking down parts of fencing, climbing through electric fencing and destroying anything that got in her way. Unfortunately Cloud was very susceptible to laminitus, so breaking into fields full of lush grass was not good.

I began to wonder if Reiki could help, I had experienced many a time the effect that Reiki could have if one visualized a large aura around themselves, with the horse paying attention, so I though about this on a bigger scale. I visualized a strong energy barrier around the paddock where Cloud was kept, imaging that it felt like a 6ft wall of energy.

I was surprised in the morning when I found that Cloud had not broken into another field, still I thought it was perhaps a fluke, only Cloud did not demolish her way out of the paddock again, so I decided that perhaps this is a very useful exercise to have and share.

Laminitis

There are many cases of laminitis and it seems many more horses are getting symptoms.

The areas I have found which seem to pull energy at a vast rate are the kidneys and liver, even if the horse is lame the organs seem to pull the energy towards them, before going to the lameness.

Reiki can really help laminitic cases, if a horse or pony is confirmed with laminitis I will treat at least 3 times a day, some of the sessions may be distant. Horse owners have noted that the horse has become sounder quicker than what was thought and that when using Reiki alongside management of diet, practitioners with laminitic prone equines were able to feel when their horses were verging on laminitis and so treat them, i.e. by keeping their diet high fibre and exercising more frequently.

The riding school horse

Merlin had been a riding school horse for 6 years before his new owner bought him. After giving Merlin 6 months to settle in, his owner felt that he was depressed and down. He seemed 'switched off' and the other horses were out casting him in the field.

I gave Merlin six Reiki treatments in total. During the first three treatments, Merlin did not respond in the usual horse way. He just stood and ignored me, I could feel energy flowing to him, however, it felt like I was treating a human not a horse.

On the fourth treatment Merlin ignored me half an hour and then suddenly let out a huge snort, it was as if he suddenly recognised something, he marched up to me and sniffed my hands, gave me a deep look and then proceeded to put his head in my hands and fall fast asleep. The next time I went to treat Merlin his owner commented that the other horses had begun to accept him. The last two treatments consisted of Merlin resting his head in my arms and falling asleep. After the sixth treatment Merlin had completely changed, his owner said that he had "become a horse, he was acting horse like and was now completely accepted as part of the herd. Merlin was happy in himself and had time for people, he paid attention to anything and everything"

Riding school horses often 'switch off' they sometimes need to preserve themselves, and so become less horse like in their mannerisms towards energy. This is something that is needed, as if all riding school horses reacted to each and every riders energy who was riding them there would be a lot more riding accidents! We need to give these horses our patience and time to allow them to feel the energy again and become one with it.

Sending Reiki to the situation

I decided to send Reiki to the situation of trying to catch my mare, remove her from the herd, out of the electric gate and back down the long lane, passing four fields to the yard. I had been experiencing several 'problems' with this.

- *The dominant mare (a young fiery chestnut – what else!) does not like the other mares to leave the field before her. I often arrive around the time they all come in for tea – so she runs at my horse to keep her away from me, and presents herself to be brought in. This can be time consuming if I 'give in' and bring her in first then go back to get my horse.*

- *I have tried waving a spare lead rope at her but she takes no notice. I've tried carrying a schooling whip but she can't feel it through her two thick winter rugs. She has been known to turn her back legs on people and kick out, so it's not a good situation. (This does happen to the other mare owners too, she knocked one lady over – she even chased the farrier out of the field on one occasion when he was turning out a mare after shoeing.)*

- *Even when I catch my mare, I have difficulty getting her through the electric gate, especially on windy days when there is the added fear of dragons and monsters in the lane (plastic bags in the trees and leaves and twigs being blown around).*

- *If I do manage to get her through the gate without being threatened by the boss mare, then Sophie tries to run back into her field when I'm trying to close the electric gate, as she is afraid of the traffic movement (the lane is next to the M62 Motorway). Neither of my hands are strong and I have very poor grip due to arthritis so sometimes I just have to let her go.*

- *If everything goes smoothly then we face the walk down the long lane to the yard. My mare turns into a lunatic, fire-breathing, demented beast, giving a good impression of a mad stallion. She grows from 15.2 to 18.2 tosses her head and skips and trots sideways and drags me off my feet.*

My horse used to be difficult to catch sometimes and I got into the habit of using HSZSN to connect with her. This really helped, so it was frustrating to be able to catch her but then have all the other problems.

So, I sent the Reiki with the intent that all went smoothly and I visualised what I wanted to happen. (In my 'perfect' scenario, Sophie was waiting by the gate, the dominant mare was far away eating grass, there was no wind and no litter, and Sophie and I walked slowly and peacefully down the lane.)

Day 1: Sophie was not by the gate – she was at the far end, right in the middle of the girls and I had to pass the 'boss' mare to get to her. They were not even eating, just standing around. I envisaged CKR symbols around myself and hoped for the best. It was as if I was invisible! None of the mares moved, I was able to catch Sophie and bring her in with no trouble at all. Cool! There was not much wind and I had removed as much rubbish as I could the day before.

Day 2: Managed to catch Sophie who was well away from the others. The dominant mare ignored us – but it was unfortunately very windy and there were new bits of plastic sheets flapping in the trees. I was unable to get her through the gate. I gave her some Reiki in the field then let her go. She pelted off to her friends. (This day was particularly windy – one of our lilac trees blew down.)

Day 3: As I walked up the lane, Sophie saw me coming and started walking to the gate. She got there before I did and then started walking away, but she just circled and circled until I got there! We negotiated the gate easily and she walked down the lane calmly, with her head low. (I was so grateful!)

Day 4: When I got to the yard all the horses were in their 'summer fields' so no long lane to deal with. To get to her field I have to go through a 'boys field' – as I walked across, there she was, waiting at the gate. The yard owner happened to be there checking the field water so he held onto the dominant mare whilst I got through the gate. Now, although there is no lane to navigate there are instead 3 electric gates. Sophie behaved beautifully through all of them and didn't even flirt with the boys on the way through their field.

Day 5 : When I arrived I could see Sophie circling by the gate! By the time I had unloaded the car and got my lead rope she was walking away from the gate. (I was 10 minutes later than I had told her I'd be there.) The boys had been moved to another field so there was one less gate to contend with. I caught Sophie easily, (apologising for my lateness with a carrot bribe) and had no trouble getting her through the gates. After riding her I also had no problem turning her back out as the chestnut mare was in, being prepared for a competition.

Day 6: Sophie was waiting by the gate, not eating. All the others were well away from the gate with the young chestnut. Again only two gates to deal with – no issues whatsoever.

Day 7: Sophie was waiting by the gate … fantastic!

N.B. These days are not consecutive days of the week, as sometimes I have to work late, (and the horses are already in) but they were consecutive 'catching' visits.

I do feel that sending the Reiki had a very positive effect. Also I noticed that once in her stable, Sophie was standing fairly still to be groomed. This is most unlike her as she usually fidgets and moves around a lot.
Elinor Mary Thomas

Healing the physical

Mill Sonador, is a 3 year old pure bred Andalusian horse. I was first asked to treat him when he was a yearling, and had been kicked on the near side hock, dislocating the joint, and resulting in bursitis, which was proving troublesome to heal, the owner called me to see if I could help with reiki.

As Sonador was a youngster, never having received reiki before, I kept the first session short, approx 25 mins.

After treating the bursitis directly with reiki, I finished by placing my hands over his heart chakra, and felt a most unusual vibrating sensation, immediately Sonador nudged me, looked me straight in the eye and "spoke" to me, saying that he knew what I was doing, and that it was ok by him.

It was not until I mentioned this to the owner, that she told me that he had been born with a heart valve defect, the valve being stuck open, but was now ok after surgery.

Following further treatments he became sound, has since passed his grading and declared fit by the vet for breaking in.
Susan Human

Veterinarians seeing results

I got the dreaded phone call saying my horse Kilkenny Lad was involved in an accident and they couldn't stop the bleeding in his leg. I had phoned the vet, he was on his way and I was racing down to the yard.

On arrival my horse was bandaged up to stop the bleeding. The vet arrived and took off the bandage to find Kilkenny lad had a large flap of skin hanging on the front of his leg and the vet didn't know if there would be enough skin from the flap to cover the wound. O.M.G. what had happened! At bringing in time the girls had heard a noise and saw Kilkenny lad heading to his stable and the rest of the horses were out of the field and walking in the yard, also the metal field gate had fallen down and everyone could only think Kilkenny Lad had been caught under the gate and couldn't get free and his leg had been getting cut while he was trying to get up. Kilkenny Lad was sedated and the vet stitched his leg and managed to stretch enough flap to cover the wound.

The vet came out the next day to see the wound and said the wound would probably break down, there would be a lot of fluid and the stitches would break. He re-bandaged and would come out in a weeks time as he was concerned about the break down of the wound.

So I gave Kilkenny Lad Reiki every spare minute I had, he had about 4-5 wraps of cotton wool with 2 bandages and 2 vet wraps around his leg I held my hands over the bandages and gave Reiki the heat was amazing. Kilkenny Lad fell asleep and enjoyed his treatment.

The vet came for his check up and couldn't believe his eyes the wound was holding together, there was no fluid and the wound was nice and clean it was looking good. I was so pleased.

I kept giving Reiki, it was amazing, the vet kept contact with me by phone told me to keep doing what I was doing and Kilkenny Lad got better. I couldn't thank Reiki enough for helping.

The vet was on our yard a few months after and I showed Kilkenny Lad's leg to him, he was so pleased with it and was glad I let him see it as he couldn't believe how well it had healed.

Linda Carr

Developing the Rider to Horse connection

My son's horse has developed so much since I started doing Reiki with him, but then again so has my son. I have worked on them both and they have become proud, honoured and most of all enjoy riding so much. My son's teachers cannot understand the reason the horse developed so much in a short while or why he is jumping all obstacles they set him to jump or how he won 1st place last month. Even my son has changed so much and is trying hard to become better each day and to get closer to his horse so they can both work as one. My heart is rejoyced in happiness to see them both doing so well, I have been blessed with an amazing son and all the horses that have come into my life.

Olivia Monteiro

When horses heal

I was dreading my riding lesson; I had hurt my back, just next to my shoulder. As I waited by Pancho's stable I decided to sit in a chair in front of the stable door, which I had left open so that Pancho could stand next to me. Sitting down didn't make me anymore comfortable and the more I thought about trying to ride with my back hurting as it did, the more tense and in pain I became.

I began to think I would have to cancel the lesson, which in turn made me feel guilty as well as in pain and tense, as the trainer had travelled a long way.

Pancho who had been quietly dosing, began to move his muzzle across my back, he stopped where the pain was and I heard him take a huge sigh, as he exhaled I felt a mass of warm heat go into my shoulder, it travelled throughout the whole of my body, in that instant the pain was gone!

When this first happened, I knew to myself that Pancho had helped, but after a few days I began to question myself – could that have really happened? Do animals have such ability to heal that they can literally relieve pain in an instant?

Needless to say, my doubts were dissolved as this has become a regular occurance, Pancho has picked up areas on many course participants and myself and has helped them to heal, whether emotionally or physically.

We have also noticed that our Spanish stallion Oceano will pick up if you have any injuries, he knows that the energy around that area is not how it should be and will nudge the area.

Horses helping humans

The first experience which springs to mind regarding Equine Reiki was when I gave Reiki to Pancho at Epona Equine Reiki Centre. During the treatment Pancho gave me a "hug". The energy and intent caused me to ball my eyes out because it was so unexpected and the tears were a release of a long suppressed sense of bereavement from always being the "carer".
Dianne Chapman

Small pets

There are many companion pets people have in their houses or gardens that would love to join in with their Reiki shares.

Ways to approach the treatment

We can approach a treatment for most small animals in a similar way

- From outside the cage

- Holding the pet in your hands

- Sitting with the animal in an enclosed room or place.

Remote Treatment – from outside the cage

Sometimes it can be easier or necessary to treat from outside the cage, for example, if you are giving Reiki to a hamster that will bite and cling onto your finger, it can be a nicer experience for you to treat from a distance!

1) Sit or stand comfortably, somewhere not too far away from the cage.

2) Close your eyes and connect to Reiki.

3) You may like to hover your hands near to the cage, or simply sit with your hands in your lap - either way is fine.

4) Allow Reiki to flow from your hands.

5) Feel the energy from the animal as he decides to connect with the Reiki you are sharing.

6) Let the Reiki flow, small animals may like a treatment for around ten minutes, however, if an animal is staying connected and the energy flow has not slowed from your hands just allow it to flow, the animal will tell you when he has had enough.

Hands on

When the circumstances allow, it is nice to be able to share Reiki with an animal hands on. With smaller animals we can either hold them in our hands, or hold them in one hand and let the other hand gently rest over their back.

One can either allow the energy to flow, just sitting quietly and sharing the moment, or you can use your intent to balance the chakras and ask where the Reiki is needed allowing Reiki to help with any issues the animals may be suffering with.

Reiki in an enclosed space.

If the animal is allowed to roam free in an enclosed and safe place I would recommend the following instructions:

1) Sit on the floor so that the animal can come as close to you as he would like to

2) Connect to Reiki

3) Begin to fill the room with Reiki, filling the room with beautiful light and good feeling.

4) Feel as the Reiki comes through your body, begin to radiate Reiki from the whole of your body, so that you are shining Reiki in all directions.

5) Keep sending Reiki until the animal has had enough, or you feel that it is time to stop.

The timid rabbit

Vicky had bought herself a rabbit. Bonny was very nervous, having only ever been picked up by his ears. Vicky brought the rabbit home and sat in a stable with  *him. Bonny was petrified, his heart was racing, his nostrils were going ten to the dozen. Vicky stroked his back thinking loving thoughts and calming energy, after five to ten minutes Bonny suddenly decided that Vicky was the best thing since sliced bread! He ran off round the stable, came back and jumped on her lap for mores strokes. Each time Vicky approached Bonny, he would jump against the wall making loud thudding sounds with his paws, showing off and unable to contain himself when she was around. As soon as Vicky entered Bonnys pen, he would jump up and try to get on her lap straight away.*

It was amazing to see how quickly the energy of love allowed this lovely little creature to feel safe and at ease. This is extremely unusual behaviour for a rabbit.

Tommy the Tortoise

Tommy had my attention as soon as I set eyes on him, there is just 'something' about turtles and tortoises which makes me want to stay and watch them.

I asked his owner if she minded me sharing Reiki with Tommy, I knew as soon as I asked that it wouldn't just be giving Reiki, it would be experiencing a connection with an old soul.

Tommy and I connected, the feeling was beautiful, I felt part of the earth, a part of a whole, protected and safe in the knowledge that we are all part of a bigger picture. The Reiki share continued for over half an hour, the whole time I knew I was being shown about life itself, I felt that I had been given something special.

As the session came to an end I thanked Tommy for what he had shown me, everything seemed so clear, life seemed so understandable, however, in that same moment the memories were gone, it seemed they had vanished from my mind, instead I was left with a feeling stored in my body, a faint realization, which brings a feeling of eternal love from the earth itself.

Reiki for Fish

The simplest way to share Reiki with fish, is to Reiki the water. You may often find that the fish will come over to your hands at the sides of the fish tank whilst you are sending Reiki.

1) Connect to Reiki
2) Place your hands on the tank
3) Allow Reiki to flow into the tank and fill the water with beautiful energy.
4) Let the Reiki flow until you begin to feel the energy slow in your hands or until you feel it is time to stop.

A fishy encounter

My first experience of giving Reiki to fish was a little strange. I had been carrying out an Equine Reiki treatment for a customer and whilst we talked about her horse she asked how fish responded, I had no idea and was very pleased when she asked me to see how her fish reacted.

I placed my hand on the side of the tank, and felt Reiki flow, three fish came over and swam next to my hand, they stayed there for around ten minutes, each having the odd swim away but coming straight back. I wondered if this was something they usually did, perhaps they were waiting for food, their owner assured me this was not the case; she said she could tell they were having Reiki.

Reiki with Farm animals

When sharing Reiki with farm animals, which may not be very tame, I have found it is best to simply allow Reiki to flow. Many a time I have sat in a field with a herd of cows, just allowing Reiki to shine from my body in all directions.  The animals will often make their way closer, sometime one in particular will come closer, other times the herd will gradually move towards you and you may feel a connection begin with a particular animal.

I have found that after visiting a herd of animals a few times they accept you as an energy sharer and so the more they will show their responses whilst you are present. So don't be disappointed if the first few times you give Reiki to farm animals, they don't respond, just give them time and patience.

Sheep on Demand

As I drove past the sheep in the field, I felt a sadness coming from them. I stopped the car and began to send Reiki, allowing Reiki to flow to wherever it was needed. None of the sheep responded in any physical way but I felt a connection with a particular ewe.

The next day as I was about to pass the field I felt the urge that I needed to stop, I listened to my intuition, stopped the car and began to send Reiki. Again none of the sheep seemed to notice what I was doing, except the ewe I had felt a connection with the previous day – she looked at me a couple of times, keeping her gaze set for a minute or two.

Day three, as I approached the field, the ewe was standing at the fence where I had stopped my car each day, I pulled over and began to send Reiki, she lay down and went to sleep.

Each day I was greeted by the ewe at the fence asking for Reiki, and each day she would fall fast asleep. After nine days of Reiki sharing I drove up to the field, the pulling had disappeared, I slowed down to look for the ewe and saw she had a beautiful baby. She caught my gaze and stared intently at me, as if to say thank you, I smiled and drove off.

Poultry plucking

I was asked to give a Reiki treatment to a chicken that was plucking her feathers

out. The owner went to catch the chicken and passed her to me to hold. I had the feeling that the chicken should be able to roam, so I asked if we could go into the pen and just relax, instead of having to try to hold on to a  chicken who didn't particularly like people. I sat in the pen and began to send Reiki, as I did this all of the chickens began to cluck, they all looked at me and clucked very loudly. The bravest chicken came towards me stopped at my feet and relaxed down, in turn each of the chickens joined and relaxed around where I was sitting.

Last to come was the chicken I had been asked to treat, she made her way up to me and relaxed against my leg. I really had not expected this reaction, it was very enjoyable and the chickens seemed to love it.

After the treatment, the owner reported that less feathers were being plucked and also she was laying eggs more frequently.

Wildlife and Reiki

When we share Reiki with the wildlife around us I would suggest the following method:

- Allow your mind to clear
- Connect to Reiki
- Feel your body relax in to the nature around you, become part of the natural beauty you are surrounded in (even if you are in a city you can think of a beautiful forest or something else that makes your body feel the nature sensation)
- Let the love for animals you have be shown through your heart, you may like to visualize your heart chakra shining brightly from your chest.
- Allow Reiki to flow around you, let the energy touch every living thing around you.

Treating wildlife is often a case of sitting back, opening up to the energy and letting the energy flow ready for the animal to join with the connection when he wants to.

Our good friend Robin

Each year Robin comes to visit, he and his wife have a lovely time chirping their way around the property. Robin has become quite keen on the Reiki course days, when we go out to treat the horses, after approximately five to ten minutes, he comes to join us. He sits at the top of the stables and sings to the course participants or sometimes hops along the alley between the indoor stables chirping away. The Reiki energy seems to really attract him and he stays throughout the treatments. One year he had a blackbird friend and they both came to join in each Reiki session – of course we had to call them Batman and Robin!

Working with Chakras

What is a Chakra?

Chakra is a Sanskrit word meaning wheel; it refers to the seven energy centers in our body. The chakras regulate the flow of energy through our energy system.

Each sense, feeling and experience is divided into seven categories and therefore allocated to a specific chakra. When a person's chakras are dull or aren't spinning properly, the emotional, physical and mental body will not be working in harmony with each other.

Balanced chakras results in optimal health and vitality.

Each of the seven main chakras is comprised of seven levels, they are:

1)   Physical

2)   Emotional

3)   Mental

4)   Causal (cause and effect)

5)   Intuitive and/ or psychic

6)   Spiritual

7)   Transcendental or beyond that of the physical realm

The Base/ Root Chakra

Security, trust, the home and work are all connected with the root chakra; the root is where life begins. This chakra also reflects a beings connection to Mother Earth

Colour – Red

Stones associated – Garnet, Ruby, Smoky Quartz

Location – Located at the base of the animal spine (near the tail)

Influences – Adrenal glands, spine, bones (marrow), legs, back feet, kidneys, colon, anus and tail.

Sense - Sense of smell is covered by this chakra

Effects of Reiki – Channeling Reiki to the Root Chakra helps to balance the physical animal body and clear out fears, insecurity and anger. Also helps to relieve spinal tension, constipation, anemia's, urinary incontinence and any related problems associated with the areas mentioned under influences.

The Sacral Chakra

This chakra is linked to emotions and your willingness to feel your emotions.

Colour - Orange

Stones associated – Moonstone, Topaz, Opal

Location – Located in the lower abdominal area

Influences – Genital, pelvis, reproductive organs, large and small intestines, stomach, sacrum and lumbar vertebrae.

Sense – The sense of taste and appetite are associated with this chakra

Effects of Reiki – Reiki helps to relieve sexual difficulties, impotence, release tension, increase male potency, heal problems with uterus or bladder and any related problems associated with the areas mentioned under influences.

The Solar Plexus Chakra

Power, control and mental activity are associated with this chakra. It is linked to personality. The power centre is connected to the solar plexus. This is the chakra from which the animals power and mastery of self originates.

Colour - Yellow

Stones associated – Tigers Eye, Amber, Citrine

Location – Located in the middle abdominal region

Influences – Stomach, gallbladder, pancreas, liver, diaphragm, kidneys, nervous system and lumbar vertebrae

Sense - Eyesight

Effects of Reiki – Reiki helps to clear digestive disorders, increase appetite, increase energy, eliminate fatigue and any related problems associated with the areas mentioned under influences.

The Heart Chakra

The heart chakra is associated with the heart and is the chakra of love and compassion.

Colour - green

Stones associated – Emerald, Green Jade, Rose Quartz

Location – Located in the centre of the chest

Influences – Heart, blood circulation, lower lungs, chest, thoracic vertebrae, immune system

Sense – Touch and the sensitivity that comes from being touched

Effects of Reiki – Reiki helps to alleviate heart and circulatory problems, immune system dysfunctions, emotional instability, anger. Energizes the blood and circulation. Instills harmony, balance, contentment, peace and happiness. Helps with other problems associated with areas mentioned under influences.

The Throat Chakra

The throat chakra is related to communication and creativity.

Colour - Blue

Stones associated – Blue Topaz, Turquoise, Aquamarine

Location – Located in the throat

Influences – Thyroid, lungs, respiratory system, forelegs, feet, throat, mouth, vocal chords

Sense - Hearing

Effects of Reiki – Reiki helps to alleviate depression, thyroid problems, vocal problems, hair loss, abnormal weight gain or loss, problems with metabolism, and any related problems associated with the areas mentioned under influences.

The Third Eye Chakra

This is the chakra of animal thinking and emotions

Colour - Indigo

Stones associated– Blue Sapphire, Clear Quartz, Tourmaline

Location – Located between the eyes.

Sense – It is related to seeing, both physically and intuitively and tunes in to our psychic ability.

Effects of Reiki – Reiki helps to alleviate headaches, problems with the eyes, tension, hyperactivity, jumpiness and any related problems associated with thinking and emotions.

The Crown Chakra

This chakra controls every aspect of the animal body and mind. It is also known as the cosmic consciousness centre. It is associated with the brain and nervous system.

Colour – Violet/ purple

Stones associated – Amethyst, Clear Quartz, Opal.

Location – Located on top of the head.

Effects of Reiki – Reiki helps to alleviate confusion, senility depression, malaise and convulsions. This chakra gives a sense of empathy and unity and is calming when centered on.

How to see the chakras

1)   Sit or stand comfortably. Close your eyes.

2)   Take a few long deep breaths and centre yourself.

3)   Feel the energy entering through your crown, coming down the middle of your body and filling your Tanden.

4)   Feel the energy building in your Tanden. We work from the Tanden.

5)   Look through your third eye and allow yourself to see each chakra.

6)   If the animal comes over to you and presents himself forward whilst you are channeling Reiki to one of his chakras, carry on sending Reiki to that particular chakra. The animal is saying; ok you've hit the spot, now I'd like it a bit closer!

People experience chakras in different ways, some see them all straight away, with breath taking colours, others see objects or symbols in the chakra and some find that they can see the chakra by imagining they open a lid or unfold petals etc and look inside to see each chakra individually.

Some chakras may appear sluggish or dull, we can send Reiki into the chakra to speed it up or make it more vibrant and the same is also possible for the opposite; if a chakra is spinning too fast or irregularly. With your hands in the prayer position or relaxed down by your sides channel Reiki towards the animal and to his chakras. You do not need to be standing with your hands hovering over the animal; we can treat the animal's chakras using our intent just as effectively from a distance as to be up close.

You do not have to be able to 'see' chakras to be able to treat them, just by using your intent to focus that you would like to bring each chakra to its optimum functioning is quite sufficient.

Location of Chakras

If one searches the internet, they may find that people have different views as to exactly where different animals chakras are. If you find that you are able to see the chakras then you can find out for yourself where they appear.

When I look at an animals chakras, I have found that they are in similar positions to a persons chakras, the energy centre fills the whole of the area that it is located, they are big and bold, spreading out of the physical body and into the energy field. There are more chakras than the seven mentioned above, however, these seven are the main ones you would be working with.

Using symbols during treatments

How to draw the symbols

Draw the symbol in your minds eye. Some people prefer to draw the symbol in violet as this is the colour mostly associated with Reiki energy, however, it doesn't matter whether the symbol is drawn in violet or just with light; it will still work. After drawing the symbol, say the symbols name silently to yourself three times. The combination of drawing the symbol and saying the symbols name three times 'activates' the symbol and produces its effects.

<u>The first symbol is: Cho Ku Rei</u>

Pronounced 'Show Koo Ray', this symbol represents Earth Ki.

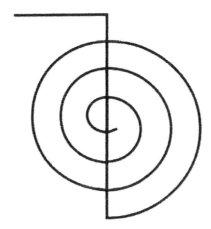

The energy from Cho Ku Rei relates to our physical body and physical reality. It is often referred to as 'The Power Symbol' as it can feel very powerful, however this does not mean that this symbol is more powerful than the others, it's energy is just different and perhaps more apparent as it is related to the physical body and we feel things with our physical body.

Drawing Instructions for Cho Ku Rei

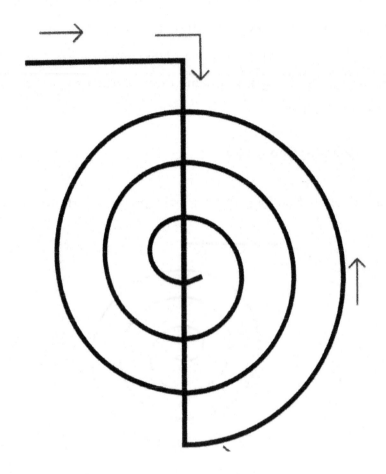

The Second Symbol is: Sei He Ki

Pronounced 'Say Hay Key', this symbol represents Heavenly Ki.

The energy produced from Sei He Ki is Heavenly energy, it relates to us in a mental, emotional and spiritual way. This is the energy of our spiritual essence and brings harmony and balance to the mental and emotional aspects of ones self.

Drawing Instructions for Sei He Ki

The left part of the symbol is drawn first (from top to bottom), then the right part (from top to bottom) and finally the two half circles (again from top to bottom).

The Third Symbol is: Hon Sha Ze Sho Nen

Pronounced: 'Hon Shay Zay Show Nen' this symbol represents Oneness.

The Hon Sha Ze Sho Nen symbol is the given way of experiencing the state of oneness. We are all one. This symbol is also seen as the distant healing symbol, being used as a way to 'connect' to others.

The HSZSN symbol is different to Cho Ku Rei and Sei He Ki as it does not produce an energy, rather it elicits a state within the practitioner; a state of oneness where you can move beyond time and space.

Drawing Instructions

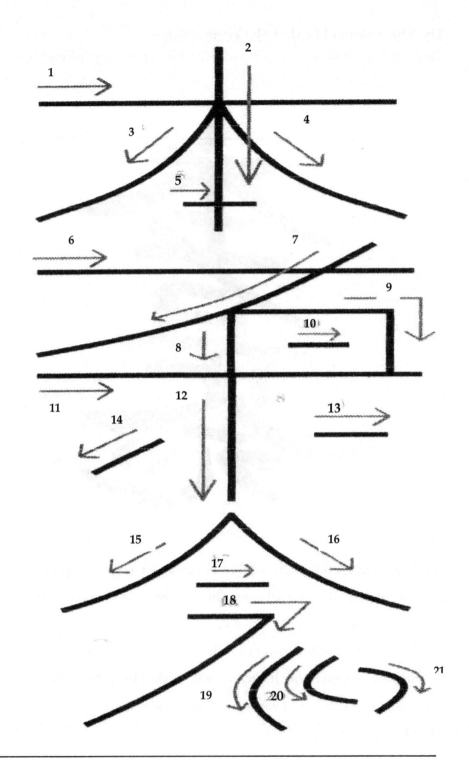

Meditating on the Symbols

Before we use the symbols on animals, we need to become familiar with their energies. We can do this by simply spending sometime meditating on each symbol individually.

The following method of meditating on the symbols should be carried out for between five and ten minutes for each symbol.

1)   Sit comfortably in your chair, rest your hands in your lap; palms facing upwards and close your eyes.

2)   Visualize one of the symbols in the air above you, say the symbols name three times, silently to yourself to empower it.

3)   As you inhale, draw energy down from the symbol. In through your crown, pulling the energy down the centre of your body to your Tanden.

4)   As you pause before breathing out, feel the energy building and becoming stronger in your Tanden.

5)   As you breathe out; flood the energy throughout your body.

You do not need to keep the symbol clear in your minds eye constantly throughout the meditation. Just by clearly drawing the symbol at the beginning and using your intent that you are meditating on this energy is sufficient.

<u>NB</u> – Your Tanden, also called the Dantien is an energy centre located approximately 3 – 5cms below your belly button and 1/3 of the way into your body.

Meditating on the Symbols; What might you feel?

People experience the energies differently, although there does seem to be a similar way in which people describe what they have felt from a particular symbol.

Generally the first symbol, Cho Ku Rei produces a denser, heavier energy. It can feel very strong and powerful in its healing of the physical body.

The second symbol, Sei He Ki tends to feel lighter than Cho Ku Rei, perhaps more gentle and wispy.

The third symbol, Hon Sha Ze Sho Nen does not produce an energy but rather allows you to experience a state of oneness. We are all one. We are connected to everything and everyone and this symbol enhances this feeling.

After a time of meditating on the symbols, or maybe even straight away, you will be able to feel the differences easily; the different way in which Cho Ku Rei and Sei He Ki feel and the state of oneness that Hon Sha Ze Sho Nen produces. Once you are at this stage you can begin to use the symbols on your treatments of others.

Using the symbols/ different energies during treatments

People use the symbols in different ways during treatments and it is up to you to experiment and find which way works best and feels best for you and the animal which you are treating. I would advise you to follow your intuition; if at some point during the treatment you feel that the animal needs Cho Ku Rei or Sei He Ki then follow your intuition and send Cho Ku Rei or Sei He Ki to the animal.

Using Hon Sha Ze Sho Nen

We can use HSZSN to help us connect and become one with the animal particularly at the beginning of the treatment. I do find that this works very well, especially on an animal that seems to be mistrusting, unsure or unresponsive to Reiki.

Do this as follows;

1) Stand quietly and allow your mind to clear.

2) Close your eyes

3) Take a few long deep breathes and connect to Reiki

4) Say to the animal by thought or out loud "take as much or as little as you would like"

5) Feel the energy flowing through your crown and down into your Tanden

6) Let the energy build in your Tanden

7) In your minds eye draw HSZSN in the air above you

8) Say the symbols name three times, silently to yourself to empower it

9) Feel yourself and the animal connect, you become one; you are no longer separate beings, you are united as one.

After using HSZSN in the initial connection process, we can carry on the treatment as usual, letting the energy flow to the animal. If you feel any stiffness/ pain or reaction in any part of your body send Reiki to this part of the animal, as this will usually be the animal showing you where to send the energy.

Using CKR and SHK during treatments

If you feel that CKR or SHK are needed during a treatment, then the following method is advised;

- You will already have connected to the animal and the energy will already be flowing.
- You feel an inclination that CKR or SHK are needed.
- In your minds eye, draw the symbol in the air above you, say the symbols name three times to empower it.
- Feel the energy from the symbol flowing down through your crown, down your body and into your Tanden.
- As you breathe out flood the energy from your Tanden through your hands and to the animal
- Carry on flooding the energy for as long as you feel necessary, or until you feel the energy flow slowing from your hands

CKR relates to the physical body, so if the animal has a physical injury, problem or stiffness you will usually find that you feel that you need to use CKR.

SHK relates to the mental and emotional state of the animal, so if the animal has a mental or emotional issue that needs addressing you will usually find that you feel that you need to use SHK.

If you prefer you can trace the symbol with your hand or finger, say the symbols name three times and then 'push' the symbol into a certain part of the animal, for example, say if an animal has a physical injury, say he has had an accident to his knee, you can draw CKR with your palm or your fingers, say the symbols name three times and then 'push' the symbol into the knee where he has been hurt, with the intention that the symbol will emit physical healing energy in that area whilst you are treating and also carry on healing the knee once you have finished the treatment.

Using Reiki during exercise

We can also use the different energies whilst we are taking our animal somewhere, say for example, riding a horse or taking a dog out for a walk. We can also use the symbol on others, for example, for horse riders at a show who may be feeling up tight and nervous. There are a few ways to do this; you can draw a symbol above your head before riding and using your intent, tell the energy to flood down though you and into the horse whilst riding. You can Reiki your tack with the intention of when the tack is on the horse the energy will take effect. Or as you are riding around you can draw which ever symbol you feel is needed, empower it and then carry on riding.

SHK is wonderful to use for people who are feeling nerves at a show or people who are getting cross and frustrated with their animals in everyday life.

CKR is especially good for people who look weak around their animal, for people who haven't control over the animal, for example, someone who looks weak on a horse, like they may have difficulty controlling the horse or a child showing a dog.

HSZSN is a good energy to help all people have a stronger bond with their animal, making all other problems disappear and reminding and allowing the body to feel completely at one with the animal. I have found HSZSN to allow the person to connect to the animal and often the person will have a sudden realization about their animal as they find that they understand him more.

Reiji Ho

Using your Intuition

Everyone has intuition and everyone is intuitive. When carrying out a treatment you already know where to put your hands on the recipient, however, our conscious mind tends to block our intuition, blocking our access to what we already know and what is already within you.

Reiji Ho is used in Japanese style Reiki, it means 'indication of the spirit technique', meaning that the energy tells you where to treat.

When you work with Reiji Ho, you will find that the harder you try to make it work, the less likely it is that it will work. Eventually you will find that using Reiji Ho will be effortless.

To perform Reiji Ho the following instructions are suitable;

1) Put your hands in the prayer position, close your eyes, feel the energy coming down through your crown, down your body and into your Tanden.

2) Feel the energy building in your Tanden

3) Move your hands in front of your third eye and say something like "please let my hands be guided to the area which needs to be treated"

4) Clear your mind and move your hands to hover over the recipient

5) Let yourself merge with the energy and allow your hands to drift

6) When your hands stop, allow the energy to flow until the feelings in your hands tell you to move on to another position. If you are unsure whether you need to move onto the next position, try taking one hand away, if you feel the hand being pulled back to the area then that area still needs more Reiki

You do not have to place your hands in front of your third eye; doing this is just seen as a ritual to connect your hands to your third eye, which is seen as the chakra associated with intuition.

You should allow your hands to drift; it will feel like magnets are pulling your hands to a particular place, they will come to rest over some part of the body. If your hands want to drift away from the body, then allow them to; Reiki may be needed to be channeled into the aura. You should not move your hands deliberately.

Using Reiji Ho with CKR and SHK

We can also use Reiji Ho in order to find where CKR (physical healing) and SHK (mental/ emotional healing) are needed;

1) Put your hands into the prayer position and close   your eyes
2) Feel the energy coming through your crown and down into your Tanden
3) Feel the energy building in your Tanden

4)	Move your hands in front of your third eye and say something like "show me where CKR is needed" or "guide my hands to where SHK is needed".

5)	Once your hands have drifted to an area and you have given enough Reiki to that area, you can repeat point 4 until you and the horse are ready to finish the session.

Using Reiji Ho in your minds eye

This technique is invaluable when using Reiki with animals, just for the fact that we can use Reiji Ho in our minds eye without having to be too close to the animal we are treating, also with animals that are mistrusting of humans, it is very useful not to have to move your real hands around them, which can upset them and also to be able to find areas which may be troubling an animal which you can not get close to.

To use Reiji Ho in your minds eye;

1)	Clear your mind

2)	Take a few long deep breathes

3)	Feel the energy entering your crown and coming down your body to your Tanden. We work from the Tanden, which is the centre of our intuition

4)	Feel the energy building in your Tanden

5)	In your minds eye see an imaginary pair of hands hovering over the animal

6) Say something like "guide these hands to where Reiki is needed"

7) The hands will move to the areas of the animal which are in need of Reiki

8) When the hands stop in a particular area you can carry on and use the imaginary hands to send Reiki to the animal. You will most likely feel heat in your own hands when your imaginary hands find the areas which need to be treated and whilst you are giving Reiki to the animal using your imaginary hands

To go one step further, we can use Reiji Ho in our minds eye, and ask where CKR or SHK are needed. To do this follow the instructions above, but when you get to point 6, say something like "guide these hands to where CKR is needed" or "show me where SHK is needed".

Distant Healing

The HSZSN symbol is also known as the Distant Healing symbol. You don't actually need to use the symbol to send distant healing but it can be used to help focus you when carrying out distant healing, by bringing you into the state of oneness deeper and in turn making it easier to reach the state of oneness required for sending distant healing effortlessly and effectively.

We can send distant healing to animals in the same way that we send it to humans. Those of you who have completed Reiki 2nd degree or above will probably already have your preferred way of sending distant healing and this approach can be used with animals.

For those who haven't encountered or practiced distant healing before, the following simple approach is how I would advise you to carry it out;

1)   Sit comfortably in a chair, rest your hands palm uppermost in your lap

2)   Close your eyes, take a few long deep breathes and centre yourself

3)   Focus your attention on your Tanden

4)   In your minds eye draw the HSZSN symbol in the air above you and say its name three times to empower it

5) As you inhale, draw down the energy of the symbol through your crown and down into your Tanden

6) Say to yourself "this is distant healing for the highest good for......................."

7) Focus your attention on the recipient in your minds eye

8) Feel yourself merge with the recipient, you become one with the recipient

9) Let the energy flow from you to them for as long as you feel necessary

10) When you feel that you are ready to finish the session; gradually withdraw your attention from the recipient, take a few long deep breathes and bring yourself back.

You will find that the distant healing treatments do not last for as long as hands on treatments. Generally each session will last for around 10 to 15 minutes, and sending distant healing everyday for 4 to 5 days.

Sending Reiki before the appointment

When you are asked to treat a client's animal I find it is a good idea to send some distant healing to the pet and his owner before the appointment. This especially works well for animals that are perhaps a little 'blocked up' and perhaps will not take very much energy on the first treatment. By sending Reiki beforehand we can 'unblock' the animal before the appointment. You do not have to do this but I have found through practice that animals are more responsive to the Reiki after they have had one initial treatment, whether this is from distant healing or you physically being there.

If you do decide to send distant healing to the animal beforehand, then I would also send some distant healing to his owner, as the animal and owner are connected and usually have the same places in need of Reiki.

To send distant healing to the animal and his owner, follow the distant healing instructions on the previous page. You do not need to know what the recipients look like to focus on them in your minds eye, instead simply use your intent to intend that the Reiki goes to the animal and owner. This will be sufficient enough to send distant healing effectively.

Remember, when we send Reiki distantly or physically in person, we are not forcing the energy on anyone but instead we are simply offering the energy to the recipients, it is up to their mind, body and spirit as to if they accept the energy, how much energy they take and what they choose to do with the energy.

Treating owners as well

Pets and their humans are connected, even if his owner does not realize it; the creature is 'one' with his human. This can be a very good thing, when a pet has a person who is in touch with their mind, body and spirit, is happy, emotionally sound and enjoys life, and then we tend to have a pet that mirrors his owners' good attributes.

On the other hand, if the pet has a human who is emotionally unstable or has underlying issues, then we will see these issues reflected in the animal. Pets mirror their humans; they mirror physically what their owners are feeling mentally and emotionally. The owner isn't a 'bad person' but as we all know, life can be hard sometimes and situations can affect us in different ways.

What I have noticed is that people who are upfront and open about any issues they have, tend to effect the animal less than people who try to be 'normal' or act 'perfect' all the time and are really lying to themselves because they are trying to hide and suppress their feelings and experiences. This sort of person will suppress something, keep it hidden and try to hide it away in part of their body, this part of their body will then 'close off', become blocked or shut down and the animal will mirror this.

To truly be at one with the animals in our lives to our best ability, and how the animal is with us, we need to be completely honest with ourselves, animals look deeply within us, they will sum you up within the first few seconds of meeting you, be honest with him; let him look deep into your soul,.

So what you will find is that the owner does really need Reiki as well as the animal, otherwise you will treat the pet, hopefully make him better and then after a few weeks or months he will start picking up his owners problems again. We can use Reiki and our intent to tell the energy we are giving to the pet that it doesn't need to pick up the problems of the owner, but really the owner does need treating as well.

Working with the animal's Aura

Every living thing has an electromagnetic field or aura around it. The aura is made of energy, someone may have a very positive aura, say for instance when you meet someone and you instantly take a like to them, knowing that they are a lovely person. Or a person may have a negative aura, the space around them being filled with all of the negative energy they create; this could be typical of someone who loves saying horrible things about people, once again, you may sense this about a person as soon as you lay your eyes on them.

Using the following exercises we can begin to work with auras, sensing them and maybe seeing them. Some people may start of sensing auras and then after a time, when they least expect it they will suddenly see someones' aura. Don't worry if you don't see colours straight away, for a while some persons can see an energy or mist and gradually after a time the colours come in to view. It is important to say here that you do not need to see anything for these exercises to work – whether you see wonderful colours and symbols or if you see and feel nothing at all, you will still be just as capable and effective at working with the aura.

I am not going to base too much emphasis on seeing the colours of the aura, there will be some information as to what certain colours may mean and examples of what one could see but first we need to focus on 'feeling the aura'. Most of you will already have felt the aura around a human or animal, it is the energy they are portraying and 'putting out' and so also the energy that they will attract towards themselves. Take some time now to see what your aura is portraying:

1)   Close your eyes and take a few deep breaths
2)   Clear your mind, let any thoughts you are having gently float away
3)   Now let your attention fall to your aura, does the energy around you feel bright and strong? Does the energy around you feel down and swamped?
4)   Write down what you feel.

Examples
Whilst carrying out the feeling your own aura exercise I first became aware of the energy around my head feeling light, I then became very aware of the energy around my Tanden being very strong and powerful
Sue

I liked this exercise; it made me more aware of the state of my aura in everyday life. I close my eyes and focus on the energy surrounding me; sometimes I will see or feel an area which is a bit depleted. I then send Reiki to my aura, so that it shines brightly in all directions. I have noticed the difference when I charge my aura; I have more energy and seem to have a better day!
Helen

It may take a few times to get to grips with this exercise, but if you just practice for a couple of minutes each day for 3 or 4 days, you will begin to feel your aura and become more aware of when you may need to send Reiki to yourself. You will begin to sense when your aura is feeling low and in turn be able to make it stronger and give your body any help it may need. It is important when treating animals to keep our energy and aura in a stable, loving condition. Animals read our aura and the energy within us the moment they meet us, so to show that we are loving, and have nice relaxing yet strong energy is an important aspect as to how the animal will accept us and want to share energy with us.

To begin sensing or feeling an animals aura we use a very similar exercise as sensing your own:

1) Close your eyes and take a few deep breathes
2) Clear your mind, let any thoughts gently drift away
3) Now let your attention focus on the energy around the animal. Looking in your minds eye, see where the aura is strong, see where the aura is depleted and closer to the body. Feel whether the energy is calm or whether the energy is dancing around all over the place.

Example

When I started this exercise I could see a haze of energy around the horse through my third eye. The energy was closer to the horse around his hindquarters, so I began to send Reiki to the horses aura. As I was sending Reiki I began to see a dull/faded red over the hindquarters, the red became brighter and began to shine as I sent Reiki to that area.

Emma

Again this may take a few attempts before you start feeling the aura, but don't give up, take your time and just 'have a go'! It is the use of your intent that is important here; just the same as when you ask to see the chakras.

The next exercise we can try is to physically feel the aura, some of you may have done this already; whilst scanning, people will usually hold their hand(s) slightly away from the recipient, they will usually find that the place where they have chosen to scan is actually on a layer of the aura, so Reiki people tend to do this anyway, even without knowing it

To feel the aura with your hand:

1) Stand or sit next to the animal, take a few deep breathes and centre yourself.

2) Keep your eyes slightly open so that you can watch where your hand gravitates

3) Hold your hand approx ½ meter away from a large animal, or around 20cms for a small animal

4) Let your hand slowly, softly drop down closer to the animal, be aware of any feelings in your hand, a magnetic pull or a slight resistance, the same sort of feeling as if you are holding a ball of energy between your hands.

5) When you feel that you have felt the edge of the aura, slowly and gently let your hand float along the back of the animal, be aware if your hand feels it can suddenly go closer to the animal, this would indicate an area where the aura is depleted.

You will most likely need to practice the exercises above a good few times before moving onto the exercise below; calming the animals aura. Practicing the exercises above will make you ready to calm an animals aura in a very short amount of time. It is an invaluable aid to be able to calm an animal quickly in any situation and one that can help you as an Animal Reiki Practitioner no end, especially when working with animals that are highly strung and very excitable.

The exercise below is appropriate when an animals aura needs to be calmed;

1) Take a few deep breaths and centre yourself.

2) Feel energy coming down through your crown, into your Tanden and building in your hand. Hold your hand out, palm facing upwards and feel the calming energy building like a ball in your hand

3) Approach the animal; let him sniff the energy in your hand.

4) Now, as you breathe out stroke down the aura on the animals neck/back a long sweeping stroke, perhaps 3 to 4 times, feeling the animal connect to your calm strong energy, letting the animal connect to you and resonate at the same energy that you are portraying.

Example

I tried this exercise on my horse when I took him to a competition, he was rather excited and to be honest I wasn't sure if it would work. I took some deep breaths, felt the energy in my hand and stroked his aura, down his neck, as I breathed out, he looked at me took a huge sigh and relaxed!

Helen

A mare we had in for stud was becoming stressed in the stable; she had only arrived a few hours beforehand and was quite highly strung. I tried the above exercise on her, at first she had no response whatsoever, I carried on and when I stroked her aura for the 5th time she exhaled in time with me and relaxed her muscles and body

Sarah

Again don't worry if you find this hard at first, you don't have to have an animal that is excitable to practice on, just trying the exercises a few times over will begin to sow the seed and allow you to connect, feel and see the animals aura.

Some animals may appear to be calm and settled when really their aura is all over the place, changing from minute to minute, these types of animals are often very depressed and have lost or are losing touch with what their energy is doing. This can be quite deliberate. Perhaps a better way to explain this is that these types of animals are becoming more 'human' in the way they control or ignore what their energy is doing i.e. they are 'putting on a show' that everything is fine, just as a human would and just as their human would be doing.

Colours: what could they mean?

After a time you may begin to see colours within the aura whilst looking through your minds eye, this is not essential but can give further clarification to an issue. You may also find that after seeing colours in the aura in your minds eye you may gradually begin to see the colours of the aura with your eyes open, this may first occur when you see someone with strong emotions, say you see someone who is very annoyed and see a glow of red around the part of their body where they are holding the anger. As this develops further you may find that you can see auras and their colours whenever you want to.

In general, the more colourful, cleaner and brighter the aura and the more constant the energy distribution in the aura, the healthier and more balanced the animal is; just as when we work with the chakras.

We are each unique individuals and colours may hold different meanings for us than for others, just as a piece of music inspires different feelings in different people. So although there may be many similarities in what a certain colour may mean, it is most important for you to feel what that colour means to you in the way in which it is being portrayed. Different tones of the same color communicate different meanings.

The colours of an animals aura are also affected by the energies of other people. It is common for animals to have their owners colors in their aura. Having someone else's energy in your aura can create many problems, including confusion, inner unrest and even health problems. To pick up the energies in the aura which are put upon the animal we use our intuition. You may suddenly get a feeling that this is not the animals own energy but that it has latched on to the animal via his owner or someone else close to him.

The aura can contain any colour variation in the universe. So it is best to try not to put the colours into a definitive category. There are some generalised themes which can help us to interpret what a colour could mean. It is most important though for you to feel what that colour means to you, let your intuition guide you as to what you feel that colour represents. These are some rough guidelines for interpreting the colour of the aura;

Red

Red can symbolize; passion, energy, strength, physical activity, courage creativity, warmth, and security. It can also be associated with aggression. Seeing red in the aura can signify materialism, materialistic ambition, a focus on sensual pleasures, a quick temper, survival, raw passion, anger, frustration, menstruation, determination, sense of importance and feeling overwhelmed by change

Orange

Orange can symbolize the individual's relationship to the external world, the needs and wants of the physical body and the ways in which these are satisfied. In the aura orange can signify thoughtfulness and creativity, sensuality, physical pleasure, emotional self-expression, creativity, lacking reason, lacking self-discipline, health and vitality

Yellow

Yellow symbolizes intellect, creativity, happiness and the power of persuasion. In the aura yellow may signify intellectual development, for either material or spiritual ends, mental alertness, analytical thought, happiness, optimism, child-like, ego driven and thinking at expense of feeling

Green

Green symbolizes money, luck, prosperity, vitality and fertility. It is also associated with envy. In the aura green can signify balance, peace and often indicates ability as a healer, peace, nurturing, new growth, fear, need for security, jealousy, envy and balance

Blue

Blue is the color of spirituality, intuition, inspiration and inner peace. It is also associated with sadness and depression (the "blues"). In the aura blue can indicate serenity, contentment and spiritual development, verbal communication, freethinking, relating to structure and organization, emphasis on business, male energies, sadness and possibilities

Indigo

Indigo is associated with psychic ability. In the aura indigo can indicate a seeker, often of spiritual truth.

Purple

Purple is associated with power, both earthly and spiritual. In the aura purple may signify higher spiritual development, wisdom, authoritative, female energies, matriarchal, sense of superiority, controlling, imagination and intuition

White

White is associated with truth, purity, cleansing, healing and protection. In the aura it can signify a high level of attainment, a higher level soul incarnate to help others, very high spiritual vibration, godly, divine, inspiration, seeing spiritual big picture and compassionate

White – cloudy

New Age or religious energy, lacking consciousness, a cover-up, denial, being 'good' at expense of being 'whole'

Gold

Gold represents understanding and luck. Remember though that nothing comes from nothing. In the aura it can represent service to others, high spiritual vibration, integrity, respect, freedom, clear seeing, integrating spirit and body, creating as spirit

Pink

Pink represents unconditional love, love requiring nothing in return. It is also the color of friendship and conviviality. In the aura it can signify balance between the spiritual and the material, self-love, tenderness, female energies, gay energies, emphasis on physical appearances, being 'nice' at expense of being 'real'

Brown

Brown is the color of the earth and represents practicality, material success, concentration and study. In the aura it can indicate "down to earth-ness" and common sense, grounding, practical, male energies, invalidating, emphasizing body and denying spirit, feeling worth-less

Black

Black is the absence of colour. It represents the unconscious and mystery. In the aura it can signify some kind of blockage or something being hidden, issues relating to death, hatred, lack of forgiveness, unresolved karma, dark intentions, shadow games, needing compassion for self

The Sacred Sounds: Kotodoma

We have already begun to work with the different energies of Cho Ku Rei, Sei He Ki and Hon Sha Ze Sho Nen, you will now be familiar with these energies. Those of you who have completed the Reiki Master/Teacher course will have already worked with the kotodoma for these energies. The kotodoma are a chant that you can either say out loud or in your head, silently to yourself. Obviously if you go to give Reiki to a clients animal and you start chanting the kotodoma out loud they may think you are a little crazy; so it is up to you to choose the circumstances where you feel most comfortable to either use the kotodoma out loud or say it silently to yourself.

Kotodoma are based on the ancient idea of the sacred power of speech and are used to: approach the divine and produce changes within the physical world. There are historical accounts of kotodoma being used to stop armies in their tracks, to kill and to heal and to control the weather… ok so we're not quite at that stage yet! But, we can use the kotodoma to promote healing physically and emotionally and produce some wonderful results.

The kotodoma are the original method that Usui taught, the symbols were only introduced as tools that one could use to quickly depict the energies with the intention that in time people would be able to leave the symbols behind and just work with the energies that they represented.

The Reiki kotodoma have four names;

1) Focus which is represented by CKR

2) Harmony which is represented by SHK

3) Connection which is represented by HSZSN

4) Empowerment which is represented by Usui DKM (Master symbol)

Pronunciation

A – aaah

O – as in rose

U – as in true

E – as in grey

I – eee

Kotodoma Name	Corresponding Reiki Symbol	The sound	Pronunciation Guide
Focus	CKR	ho ku ei	hoe koo ey eee Ho rhymes with so, dough Ku rhymes with too, loo
Harmony	SHK	ei ei ki	ey eeee ey eeee keee

			ki rhymes with see, bee
Connection	HSZSN	ho a ze ho ne	hoe aaah zay hoe neigh ze and ne rhyme with play, say, may
Empowerment	Usui DKM	a i ko yo	aaah eeee coe yo ko and yo rhyme with so, go, flow

The kotodoma can be used instead of the Reiki symbols. So instead of using energy from SHK, you could repeat the Harmony kotodoma three times, or endlessly, to produce the energy. One kotodoma or energy should be used at a time, in other words you shouldn't mix the energies.

To become accustomed to using the kotodoma it is recommended that you work with the kotodoma on yourself first, below is a meditation for experiencing the energies of the Reiki kotodoma;

1) Sit comfortably, close your eyes, take a few deep breaths and clear your mind.
2) Let your attention fall to your Tanden
3) Chant the kotodoma on each out-breath, using a deep, resonate voice.
4) Vibrate the kotodoma from your Tanden, resonate the sound through your whole body, become the sound.

5) Continue for a few minutes, when you have finished chanting, just be still and let yourself experience the energy, the ripples that continue for a while.

6) Stay in this state for as long as you feel appropriate.

Practice with each kotodoma, whether it be the Focus kotodoma for a few days, then going on to the Harmony kotodoma and so on. If you trained with Mikao Usui you would have chanted each kotodoma for 6-9 months before moving on to the next, to fully assimilate that energy, to become that energy.

Once you feel comfortable and confident in using the kotodoma it is time to experiment using the kotodoma during animal Reiki treatments. Here is suitable exercise that you can use;

1) Make yourself comfortable

2) Centre yourself and let your mind become clear

3) Focus your attention on your Tanden

4) Take a few deep breaths in and out

5) Begin to chant one of the kotodomas, either out loud or silently to yourself. You may wish to chant the kotodoma 3 to 10 times and then stay quiet or you may wish to carry on the chant throughout the treatment – this is entirely up to you.

Animals tend to respond well to the use of the kotodomas, many horses I have worked with have seemed to 'recognise' the sound as if you were saying their name. People often find that using the kotodoma feels more intense and stronger than using the Reiki symbols.

The Focus kotodoma is brilliant to bring an excited animal 'back down to earth' and for physical injuries.

The Harmony kotodoma can bring great inner peace to the animal when he is displaying signs of emotional turmoil and stresses.

The Connection kotodoma can bring about a wonderful connection between animal and human, strengthen the bond and understanding. It can also be used to begin a treatment to help you connect to the animal.

The Empowerment kotodoma brings a strengthening factor, an empowering of the animals soul and spirit.

Examples
I tried using the Connection kotodoma to enable a deeper connection with the horse, I found that the horse connected to me quicker than he usually would have and when he connected to me it felt as if we were on a different level
Emma

The kotodoma are wonderful, I have practiced with the Focus and Harmony kotodomas whilst riding; I used the Focus kotodoma before a Show Jumping round, just chanting it silently to myself (so that the other competitors didn't think I was crazy!). My horse jumped really well, he was really on the ball and focused on what we were doing. After the success of the Focus kotodoma, I tried using the Harmony kotodoma on my other horse who becomes emotionally stressed in the warm up ring – she was like a different horse, staying connected to

what I was asking and there was no taking off or spinning round when other
horses went by
Helen

Soul Healing

The Empowerment kotodoma represents the DaiKoMyo (DKM) which is also known as the Usui Master Symbol. It represents the 'key to the light', creative energy, regenerative energy, the energy of rebirth. The essence of earth and heavenly energy and ultimate being.

The Empowerment kotodoma can be used within Reiki treatments, although it would be best to be used for specific situations, when your intuition tells you that this energy is what is needed. The symbol produces high frequency energy that does not deal directly with the physical, emotional or mental aspects of a person. Rather it works at the level of the soul or spirit. Using this energy during a treatment could be seen as flooding the animal with divine love or divine light.

The type of animal you may find that you would like to use the Empowerment kotodoma would tend to be one that is being eaten up inside, deep down, by thoughts and emotions, these may be the animals own feelings or they may be reflected from his owner, some examples are below;

- Self-destructive behaviour, for example, self harming
- A lack of wanting to be here in this realm
- Hate or anger towards humans, animals or themselves

When using this energy I have found that it may be too much for the animal, on his first treatment to start straight away with soul healing, rather I have felt that it is best to start with a normal Reiki treatment, whether you just channel energy towards the animal for the session, or use one of the other symbols or kotodoma. After the animal receiving a couple of 'normal' treatments, you may then find that you feel he would benefit from the use of the Empowerment kotodoma.

To use the Empowerment kotodoma as a soul healing aid the following instructions are appropriate;

1) Make yourself comfortable
2) Take a few deep breaths and focus on your Tanden
3) Feel your connection to Reiki becoming stronger.
4) Begin to chant the Empowerment kotodoma "a i ko yo" on each out-breath
5) Chant the kotodoma 3 to 10 times, or when you feel that the energy is suffice.
6) Feel the ripples of energy around you and the animal, let yourself become the energy. Just stand and feel.

Example

I experimented with this exercise on my friends rescue horse, I could feel as a massive blockage seemed to leave the horse, as this happened the horse lay down in the stable and went to sleep. After this the horse made a lot of progress, seemingly much happier and friendly towards humans

Jane

When using the Empowerment kotodoma or DKM symbol we are directing energy towards the soul. There is a lot of controversy as to where the soul is located and I would recommend that you don't try to direct the energy to any particular place, just let it flow.

Empowering the animal

The owners energy can affect the animal greatly, whether it be for good reasons, for example, people with great love for animals or the opposite. The emotions of the owner are reflected by their animal friends, the more the owner tries to hide and subdue their emotions, keeping them locked away; the more the animal will physically and mentally mirror these emotions. Personally, I believe that animals are here to teach people, they help a person along their path, to find an equal balance, to show a person what they are feeling inside – even if the owner can't see it inside themselves, the animal will show it to them – the animal will mirror the true feelings and desires of his owner, not the person they may pretend to be. Sometimes though, the animal may need help from an outside source, Reiki for example, and empowering the animal is a wonderful way in which we can aid.

Other examples of animals that may benefit from this empowerment are: horses which are stabled constantly; including some show horses and some stallions. Animals that would naturally live in a pack or herd but are kept alone missing out on the interaction and energy from the pack, the animal may have a sense that he doesn't 'belong' to any pack or herd even if there are other animals in the near vicinity. Animals that are kept alone and do not have a close connection with other animals need their human to portray a good energy and share energy with them. A lot of good horsemen and animal trainers aren't actually aware of the energy they share with their animals and how important it is, but the love they portray and the feelings they send out towards their animals keeps him with an even and positive energy level, similar to that of how fellow animals would make him feel.

It has become apparent to me that sometimes an animal may need to disconnect from his owner for a time in order to restore his energy to a balanced level. Sometimes a Reiki treatment isn't enough, it restores the energy balance for the time of the treatment but as soon as the animal comes into contact with his owner again, the energy is disrupted instantly and one would think that he had not received a Reiki treatment.

This sort of case is very rare, however, it is something I would like you to be aware of. When approached with this case I asked for guidance as to the next step and was subsequently guided through an empowerment for the animal which would help him keep his own energy and not be drained by those around him. The empowerment is as follows;

1) Stand away from the animal, quiet your mind and connect to Reiki
2) Put your hands in the prayer position and say a silent affirmation to yourself "help this animal in the necessary way" or "empower _____ to keep his energy strong to help his owner further along his/her path"
3) Now, let your hands hover near your Tanden, one over the other, palms facing your Tanden
4) Breathe in and feel the energy flooding into your body, feel the energy build in your Tanden and spread throughout your body
5) As you breathe out visualize golden light emanating, shining, radiating from your body
6) Let this build for around 10 breathes

7) Now, send energy to the crown area of the animal, see the energy spreading down through the animals body, all the way to his root chakra, hold this position for around 10 seconds or for how long you feel appropriate

8) Move on to the throat, visualize golden energy entering the throat area from all sides, channel energy for how long you feel appropriate

9) Move on to the heart, visualize golden energy, filling the heart area with love from all directions; opening the heart to love and be loved.

10) Finally channel golden energy to the solar plexus area, from this point gradually fill the whole of the animals body with golden light, then spreading out to his aura, so that he to is radiating golden energy

Examples

The empowering the animal exercise was beautiful. I could see the golden energy shining from me. Before I started to flood Reiki into the particular areas of the horse I could already see the horse begin to glow with golden energy surrounding her. I stayed like this for a few minutes, just watching through my minds eye. As soon as I had finished the empowerment she woke up and looked straight at me, as if to say thank you.

Helen

I found it hard to visualize golden light at first, but after practice this became easier, until gradually it felt very natural. When using the golden light I felt as though the Reiki was stronger. I used the empowerment on my horse with the

intent of empowering him for exercise, wow! He gave me such a wonderful ride afterwards; we were in pure partnership, he knew what I wanted as I was thinking it and gave it to me in a relaxed, attentive manner.

Jane

This is a very powerful treatment for an animal and the Reiki channel; it produces some wonderful effects, and after sharing this empowerment with an animal one will find that there is always a special connection between practitioner and animal.

Asking for guidance

At some point during your Reiki treatments you may find that you are unsure as to what to do in a certain situation. You may have noticed on the empowerment exercise above that I mention that I asked for guidance. It is up to you how you would like to think of asking for guidance; you may feel that you are connecting with your higher self or connecting with a spirit guide. The exercise below details how one would ask for guidance;

1) Close your eyes and take a few deep breaths
2) Let your mind clear
3) Keep your mind clear for a few minutes
4) Ask the question you wish to or the situation you need guidance on
5) Listen
6) You may find an answer comes straight away or perhaps you need to wait a few minutes, you may see a particular symbol, or your hands may be guided to a particular place or you may feel a particular energy to use

Becoming the animal

The meditation we will be discussing shortly is very useful for animals that are having a reaction to a particular circumstance, this could include anything from reacting badly to the start bell in the competition ring, being worried to go into small or confined spaces, to showing nerves around other animals.

By feeling what the animal is feeling in the situation we can have a greater understanding of what his body feels before he reacts and then send Reiki to the parts of his body which make him react in that way. This meditation is as easy to complete distantly as it is in the company of the animal. The exercise below is an example of becoming the horse, this exercise can easily be adapted for any animal you are treating;

Meditation to 'become' the horse;
   1) Close your eyes, take a few deep breaths,
   2) Clear your mind, let all thoughts float away
   3) Connect to Reiki
   4) Feel your body begin to glow with the build up of energy, allow the energy to shine from every part of your body.
   5) Carry on letting your body emit beautiful, calm, loving energy for around 5 - 10 minutes
   6) When you feel ready ask the horse permission to feel what he is feeling, to spiritually enter his physical self
   7) Now imagine an energy within you, a light wispy energy, rise up through your body and out through your crown

8) Let this energy go to the horses crown chakra and then down in to his body

9) As the energy enters the horses body it gradually expands

10) As the energy fills the horses body, your body becomes the horses body, you are inside the horse, let your self expand to his shape, your legs become his legs, your body becomes his body, your arms become his forearms, your neck becomes his neck, your head becomes his head.

11) Take note of how you feel inside the horse, physically and emotionally

12) Now visualize the horse at say, the competition arena, you are still there inside the horse feeling how it feels to walk on his feet, feeling how his rider sits on his back

13) Become very aware of the feelings you may now receive in your body and listen to the competition 'start bell' ring or buzz

14) Feel what this does to the horse, how it makes him feel, how loud it sounds, how his body consequently reacts and how his rider then reacts to him

15) Once you have felt this we can then go on to treat the areas that are needed, so say in this case, before the bell went off, the horse could feel his riders anticipation, which made him ready to react, the sound of the bell to the horse sounded like an aeroplane flying over rather than just a bell, the horses heart was pounding, his blood rushing, he had to react in some way and jumping 4 foot in the air seemed the right thing to do.

16) The next step is to send Reiki to each of the feelings the horse had, whilst still in his body, so we go back to the competition arena, we

already know when, where and why the horse is going to react so we can send Reiki before; as the rider tenses we send Reiki through the horses back , to the points he feels the tensions through, we then send Reiki to the issue of the bell, we send Reiki to 'block out' how loud the bell seems, we think of enjoying the sound the of the bell right through our body, as the bell sounds Reiki will already be flowing around the heart and body to keep things even, feel yourself breathing deeply relaxing your body. You may have to go through this process 3 or 4 times in a row before the horses body feels completely calm throughout the whole process. Just gently carry on until he feel calm and able to cope with the situation without his body reacting severely.

17) When you are ready to finish the treatment, thank the horse and then gently leave his body, see the wispy energy leave through his poll area and come back in to you through your crown

Example

I had been asked to treat a friends horse, which she had recently bought who had an issue with narrow gaps, for example, walking through gateways and stable doors. I carried out the exercise above and 'became' the horse as he went through a narrow gateway. I could feel that he was ready for the gate to bang into him and then I saw a picture of a gate hitting him, perhaps being blown in the wind, I also had the feeling that this had happened quite a lot of times. I sent Reiki to the situation and also sent Reiki to the area around the gates on the premises and his stable door. When I had finished the treatment I told his owner what I had felt, she hadn't thought of this and was presuming he was being naughty, as his last owners were very inexperienced and she thought he had learnt to walk all over them. After the treatment the horse had improved a lot, staying a lot calmer whilst moving through gateways and his owner was a lot happier too, as she felt that she understood him more and treated him with patience instead of becoming cross.

Sue

It may be hard when first practicing this exercise to remember exactly what to do, however, the process is not set in stone, our aim is to 'become' the animal in his stressful situation and help him to a higher degree, so just practising to become the animal without going to the stressful situation is good practice for you.

Communication

Anyone can communicate with animals, it is a gift that each of us is born with, but is gradually forgotten and unlearned through conditioning and beliefs.

We have already discussed the aura and its importance, but there is more to it yet! The aura or electromagnetic field holds every bit of information about us; everything that has happened to us in our lives and everything that is going on right now. With practice we can read the information contained in the aura, just like opening a book up and reading a story – amazing isn't it!

Some of you may have already had some form of communication with animals, seeing pictures, or feeling pain in an associated part of your body.

We receive information from animals in different ways:
- Clairvoyance: seeing pictures
- Clairaudience: hearing
- Clairsentience: feeling emotionally and physically
- Clairambience: smell or taste

To communicate successfully with animals all you need to be able to do is have a clear and open mind; letting go of any preconceptions. Through the practice of Reiki we already know how to clear our minds, so inevitably, all we need to do is ask a question and listen. Sometimes we may not need to ask a question, just showing the animal that we are here, right now, in no rush and are ready to listen will bring about a communication session.

It may take a few sessions of practice to be comfortable and confident enough to listen fully to the horse, so practice is the key. Try sitting comfortably some where and clearing your mind, let any thoughts gently float away, let your mind stay completely clear for 5 to 10 minutes and then when you feel ready picture the animal in your minds eye that you would like to communicate with, ask him if there is anything he would like to show or tell you. Don't worry, if you don't get anything for the first few times, just practice clearing your mind. You can communicate with all animals using the same techniques.

Exercise: Clearing your mind

-   Find somewhere to sit in a quiet place where you will not be disturbed. Turn off any phones and televisions or anything that may distract you.
-   Close your eyes and let your hands rest comfortably in your lap.
-   Take a few long deep breaths. As you breathe in through your nose feel the air filling your lungs, filling right from the bottom of your lungs. As you breathe out through your mouth, completely empty your lungs.
-   Now it's time to go through your body. Start with your head, feel your head becoming easily held and comfortable on your body. Go down to your neck and shoulders, perhaps shrug

your shoulders and as you do allow all the tension held from here upwards to disperse. Carry on down your body, become aware of your heart beat, feel any tension in your back and torso disperse as you focus on relaxing these parts of your body. Go further down your body, to your thighs, again feeling them relax as your focus is put on them, and then down to your knees, calves and feet. Feel your feet making a firm connection to the ground. Feel an even weight on each foot as your whole body becomes relaxed.

- Now that you have removed most of the tension held in your body, focus on your breathing again. Take three or four long, deep breathes in and out.

- Allow all worries to gently fade away. If anything comes into your head just gently usher it away. In this moment you are free from any worries or anxieties that already exist in your life. These aren't relevant here. They can just be quietly ushered away.

- Allow yourself some time to enjoy a clear and quiet mind.

When you ask a question to the animal it is important that you put the feeling of the question across, so we are not just asking with empty words, we are asking through the feelings we are portraying as well. Keep questions positive, you will get more response.

Examples of questions to ask:

Question	Examples of what you may see/ feel
What is your favourite food?	You may feel your mouth begin to salivate, hear the crunching of a certain food or see a picture of a feed bowl
Who is your best friend?	This could be any animal or human, you would most likely see a picture
What is your favourite type of exercise?	You may get a sense of freedom, like galloping in the wind for horses, or running with a pack for a dog, cats often like to show their agility.
How does your tack feel whilst you are being ridden?	If there is a problem with the horses tack you will most likely feel a pain in some area of your body, don't discount it if you feel a pain in your neck or part of your body where the tack doesn't sit, as if the horse is uncomfortable with his tack he will hold tension in other places within his body as well
Is there anything in your life that you dislike?	You may see a picture of a dog that the horse isn't keen on. You may get

	a taste or smell of something he dislikes in his food.
Is there anything that can be done to make you happier?	Animals that are happy with their lives will often send a message across that feels like "don't ask stupid questions" or a picture of food!
Is there anything you would like me to tell your human?	This often comes across through clairaudience, you may hear a voice, the voice may sound like your own or may be different, or you may see something similar to a video clip.
If the animal has an injury, ask him how it happened	You may see a video clip, say of a horse being kicked or a dog having his paw stepped on

Keep a record of the questions you ask and the answers you receive, often at first, you may receive an answer but can't quite remember everything you felt, saw or heard, so it is useful to jot down an outline of the communication which you can add to later if more comes back to you.

If you have friends with animals ask them if they would like you to practice a communication session, you can write down any experiences or information you receive and ask them to comment on your findings. This can help build confidence. It is sometimes easier to communicate distantly, just like giving a Distant Healing Reiki session, this way you won't be disturbed and won't be distracted by the cold or what the horse is doing. Some people may find it easier to have a photo of the animal they are doing the communication with, however, you don't actually need one, just your intent on the animal in question is enough to give a good communication session.

Below is an example taken from one of my clients

<u>*Questions*</u>

- Are you feeling any discomfort anywhere?

His head feels like it is whirling, like he has a headache. I have sent some healing to him.

- Is there a reason why you act differently when your rider loses her balance?

I can't seem to help it, I just panic. Flash is showing a repeated picture of him being lunged in tight side reins or draw reins, he panics and rears up, loses his balance and falls down hard. This series of pictures seems to be engrained in his memories and he acts accordingly when he feels he is going to lose his balance he completely panics.

- Could you try to stop when you feel your rider lose balance? This way she will be able to correct herself and not scare you further.

I am getting a feeling that he will really try but it may take time for him to 'think stop' when he is scared.

- Is there anything you would like me to tell your owner?

All will be alright in time. He wants you to feel happy riding him and not to worry about him all the time. When you worry, he worries. Flash is also showing me that he has a very deep connection with you, he is a part of you, he expresses the part of you that is insecure and unsure. He is so connected with you that he knows how you are feeling all of the time, not just when you are around him, but all of the time, even if you were in a different country, he would know how you were thinking and what you are thinking.

Areas found on body scan

Flash's head came up on the body scan as well as his offside shoulder and hip.

Comments:

Flash seemed a very nice chap, he cares about you deeply and is happy to have you as his human. He does want you to be happier with life and in yourself, and he too will reflect this in his behaviour when you become happier.

Feedback from animals owner:

I don't know all of Flash's history, but he did go to a breaking yard to be backed. When he came back he changed in himself slightly, a bit untrusting and I felt something had happened. I actually had a complementary therapist out to him a few months ago and he said the same; that something had happened to him in draw reins! Hopefully we can work together to help Flash trust me completely whilst being ridden.

Thank you very much

The Heart Chakra symbol: Shi Ka Sei Ki

This symbol deals with emotions directly; it produces a specific energy relating to emotions and is often used on the heart. Using this symbol could be seen as flooding the horse with love. Although generally used on the heart it can be used on other areas as well; I use this energy on the places on the horse where he is holding his emotions or has an emotional blockage. Once you are familiar with the symbols energy you can begin to use the energy directly without having to draw the symbol; the same as we already do with CKR, SHK and HSZSN.

This symbol is different to SHK in that SHK deals with the emotional and spiritual aspects of the horse. Shi Ka Sei Ki just represents the emotional, so we deal with emotions directly.

You can practice meditating on this symbol yourself to become familiar with the energy. Just draw the symbol in the air above you, say its name three times to empower it and let the energy flow down on to your crown and into your body.

Pronunciation: Shi Ka Sei Ki is pronounced 'shee kuh [as in **cup**'] say key'

Drawing instructions for Shi Ka Sei Ki

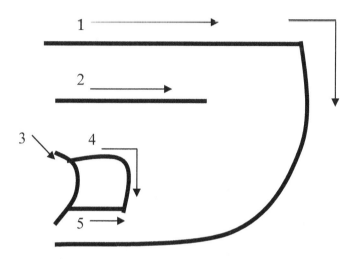

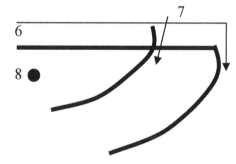

Examples

I practiced meditating on the Heart Chakra symbol everyday for a week. I expected it to have a similar feel to SHK and in some ways I felt it did but there was definitely a difference; it felt light yet really strong. I could feel a lot of heat around my heart. After a few times of meditating on the symbol, I could feel the energy building in my heart and then spreading throughout my body, I then began to cry, I could feel that I had released something emotionally, although I was crying I felt very calm and relaxed. It was very beautiful.
Sue

I used the Heart Chakra symbol whilst carrying out Reiji Ho; I asked where the energy was needed and let my hands be guided. My hands were guided to the horses neck, between his wither and shoulder blade; his owner then told me that he had been holding himself stiffly in his neck whilst being ridden and that he had started doing this after his friend had been moved to a different yard. After 3 Reiki sessions his owner noticed a vast improvement during ridden work and he felt back to his usual self.
Emma

The power of nature

Nature is powerful and beautiful. Before Reiki came into my life, I used to connect to nature to help heal, for example, I noticed that the powerfulness of a thunderstorm could be felt through the body and this energy could be 'harnessed' to help heal myself and others.

I noticed that sitting and clearing your mind by the roots of a tree allowed the body to become at one with the energy of the earth.

I found that whatever the weather, you could tune into the power of nature to help with healing qualities – the power of the sun, the force of the wind, the ability to wash away negativity and pain with the rain.

This is a practice which I still intuitively use in my Reiki sessions and I would like to share with you a meditation to connect with whichever source you would like to, for example, the earth, the sea, the moon, the sun and any other weather elements.

1) Sit or stand quietly. Allow your mind to become still.

2) Become aware of your body, on each exhale let any tension gently release.

3) Become aware of your surroundings, listen to the sounds around you, whilst still keeping your mind clear, so for example, if you are listening to a thunderstorm, just listen – try to allow any thoughts which label the thunderstorm to disperse. Just listen, be there in that moment, so that your senses and body are truly feeling what nature is giving.

4) Allow your body to connect with the elements of nature, feeling the power right through your body, feel as it invigorates your energy, passing through your body, you are sharing energy with everything around you.

5) Be still and allow the powerful healing qualities of the earth bring your body to a higher level, whilst in return your body shares and strengthens the wonderful earth energy. You are at one sharing with your soul and nature.

I hope you enjoy the above meditation. By practising connecting to earth and the elements of nature we can help improve our sense of oneness as well as feeling the energy of the earth.

Acceptance

Reiki is not always going to bring about the cure to an animals ailments. If it is the animals time to go, Reiki may aid with his passing.

As persons whom work with healing energy, the universe sometimes puts us in situations, we are in the right place at the right time, to help in the way we are needed. We aren't always needed to cure. Death is only found negative because of our thought processes about it. Reiki helps with what is needed at the time, so if an animal is passing we can aid with the pain and passing over process, simply by being there and helping the animal relax and pass, feeling safe and secure

The Ewe

Thirty minutes early for an appointment, 50 miles from home and nowhere to park! I looked for somewhere to turn the car round and found a road to a Hall, with fields either side. The road was single track with nowhere to turn easily, so I drove up for a while then turned round. In one of the fields was a sheep, away from the others, with a pink sac emerging from under her tail. "Oh brilliant", I thought, "I'm going to see a lamb being born!" I parked the car, got out my camera and went to watch.

The ewe was standing still and heaving but the pink sac kept retreating into her body. This carried on for a while and the ewe looked exhausted and nothing much was happening. I put down the camera and started sending her Reiki – she turned and stared at me (I don't suppose she'd heard the Precepts in Japanese before!)

then flopped down and lay on her side. More pushing and heaving but the pink sac was not showing any movement.

In general sheep are best left to their own devices, but I felt she needed help, so I ran back to the car and changed my high heels and best coat for my spare riding gear and a towel. I climbed over the fence and, still sending Reiki, I got hold of the sac and pulled it out the next time the ewe strained to push – the lamb came out backwards (head last) and was dead. Even though I removed the membranes, cleared its mouth and nose, held it upside down to drain the lungs, and rubbed its body, I knew it was useless.

I put the lamb next to the ewe and gave them both Reiki using SHK. The ewe licked the lamb's head twice then ignored it. Tears were rolling down my face as I stroked the ewe's head and told her that there was a reason, somewhere, for this – maybe she would be needed to foster a lamb whose mother dies? I think I was trying to reassure myself as much as her. She did not seem outwardly distressed.

The farmer arrived and said he knew the ewe had aborted and there was another twin lamb to be removed. He set about his work and I had to go to my appointment – now very late and probably quite smelly.

The ewe was on my mind constantly, so I sent her and the lambs distant Reiki (with SHK) that night and every night for the next two weeks. It was absolute chance that I was anywhere near her field at that time and although it was by no means a 'fairy tale' outcome, I know that on some level the Reiki will have helped her and I'm so glad I was there.

Elinor Mary Thomas

Feeling the Recipients pain

When I began giving Reiki treatments I realised that I was able to feel the recipients pain in my own body.

I found this very helpful whilst sharing Reiki with horses, I can feel which area is hurting or if they are afraid I can feel where they are holding the emotion in their body and so give Reiki.

During an Equine Reiki session the pain which I feel disappears when I start treating the area, or as soon as I walk away. However, when I gave treatments to people I found that I could quite easily walk away with the pain which may follow me around for the next day or so.

Why does this happen? Well some people might say that I am using my own personal energy in some way and not Reiki, leaving my energy open to be affected by others or perhaps I wasn't disconnecting properly afterwards. This could be true, but I feel that it is another way in which my intuition guides me, in fact a very helpful way.

At first I wasn't too worried about feeling a persons pain in my body, however, it became a bit taxing when I would be standing with a group of people, all with different ailments – I could end up feeling a bit under the weather to say the least!

This is when I decided to take control, I said to myself "I don't want to feel this" – and it was gone! I realised that I was in control; I can easily switch it on and off as I wish. Now I simply ask to feel where the pain is when I am treating a person and for it to be gone when I'm finished, it really is that simple. I have had many course participants ask me this question and they can not believe how simple it is to tell your intuition when and where you want to feel, for example, I am always 'switched on' to feel what an animal is feeling but I am 'switched off' to human pain unless I ask or if there is a greater need.

Believe in yourself: have confidence

Many practitioners have worries and doubts about their ability to channel Reiki or make a difference when they first start treating clients. Ok you may have carried out treatments on friends and family but treating others can seem quite daunting.

Please don't let any worries you may have put you off. The best way to overcome this is to get out and start treating people or animals. Reiki Practitioners often feel more confident after treating animals as you can see the energy having an effect; with the animal becoming calm, showing signs of relaxing and often dropping off to sleep.

If you need more confidence in yourself it is good to 'play' with the energy, try Reiki on something new everyday for a week. For example;

- Day 1 you could fill the rooms in your house with Reiki,
- Day 2 you could send Reiki to your journey to work,
- Day 3 give Reiki to your children to help them get to sleep,
- Day 4 send Reiki in the evening with the intent that you'll wake up in the morning full of energy and ready for the day ahead.
- Day 5 send Reiki to a situation which is bothering you or which you are worried about
- Day 6 send Reiki to your day, with the intent of giving you a nice, easy and relaxed day, where everything falls into place easily
- Day 7 send Reiki to the process of cooking your meal, plus all of the ingredients

Each day write down any findings you have; how was your journey to work? How was your meal? The points that you write down can be looked at each day to inspire your confidence to come through.

Although the above way of building confidence can gradually allow you to be believe in yourself, the following meditation can really help to clear doubts:

- Close your eyes, allow your mind to become clear and connect to Reiki,
- Allow your doubts of being able to do Reiki rise, ask to feel these doubts and greet them as they surface.
- Allow yourself to really feel these doubts - don't try to block them out, really feel them, feel if there is a particular place in your body where they are residing.
- By really feeling your doubts you are able to accept them, once you have accepted them, they don't affect you - they don't affect you because you have accepted that your thoughts are just a part of you, they don't control you.

It is what some call the 'negative ego' rising in you saying "you can't do this, you're not special enough", when this feeling rises smile at it, you have recognised it for what it is - which is just a thought, it is not a reflection of your abilities, it is just a thought and you as a person have the ability to control your thoughts.

Asking the universe

As Spring arrives we are inundated with beautiful swans; along the dykes around our property and opposite on the fishing lakes. I have always loved watching these magnificent birds.

When I first started writing this book, I was pondering the sort of pictures I would like to include, one which seemed to resonate, was a picture of me next to the lake with a swan, I could see this picture clearly in my mind and it bought a feeling of joy inside, however, I knew this wasn't possible, as the swans come here to nest and are always protective, not wanting people near to them.

A couple of weeks later, my partner and I took our children to a nature reserve. Whilst we walked around the pretty lake we admired the

different species of birds. We came to an opening in some trees where a swan was near, as we approached the swan came closer, I crouched down near the lake and the swan came right over – I felt honored as we shared Reiki and my partner took a picture.

That evening I looked at the picture and saw it was just as I had seen in my minds eye a couple of weeks previously!

Manifestation Exercise

Manifestation and the Law of Attraction work hand in hand – what we put out we get back. So say for instance we are thinking negatively about situations, this will attract more negativity to those situations. If you think 'I hate going shopping, it is always so busy and I can never find a parking space' then this is what you create for yourself, you have put in a special order to the universe asking for a very busy shopping centre and nowhere to park!

To attract what we would like in our lives we need to send out thoughts and images of us in that situation – not in a needy way, like you need lots of money, but in a way of feeling that you already have it. For example, when you think of the busy shopping centre with nowhere to park, it is easy for you to feel as if you were there right now, in this moment, caught up in all the hustle and bustle, your body responds at just the thought; you can live it and feel it. We need to take this approach with attracting what we would like into out lives, below is a suitable exercise for manifesting a car parking space:

- Connect to Reiki
- Allow yourself to relax
- Allow any feelings in your body to subside, breathe deeply and feel yourself relaxing further
- Visualize the parking space you would like to be free next time you go somewhere
- See yourself smile, seeing that it is free, happiness resonates through your body

-   See yourself drive into the space and again feel the laughter as you realise that the exercise worked.

You can change the above meditation, to attract anything you would like. Most people find it hard to attract the things they really need as they are perhaps too emotional whilst thinking about these things or maybe they don't really feel that they deserve luxuries, meaning that really they wouldn't be feeling that they were in that situation.

Veterinary Approval

Before you treat an animal with Reiki, the owner must first gain Veterinary approval for you to do so. The Veterinary Surgery Act 1966 prohibits anyone other than a qualified Veterinary Surgeon from treating animals, including diagnosis of ailments and giving of advice on such diagnosis. It is only legal to give Reiki to animals if you have prior consent from the owners Veterinary Practice.

The owner of the animal should gain consent before the treatment, all they need do is ring their Vet before the treatment and gain consent. I have not yet encountered any Veterinarians who do not allow Reiki treatments.

The Protection of Animals Act 1911 requires that if an animal clearly needs treatment from a Veterinary Surgeon the owner must obtain this.
To give emergency first aid to animals for the purpose of saving life or relieving pain is permissible under the Veterinary Surgeons Act 1996.

Insurance

Below are two popular insurance companies for Reiki Practitioners who choose to also work with animals:

Towergate Professional Risks

Tel: 0113 391 9555

Email: professionalrisks@towergate.co.uk

Web: www.towergateprofessionalrisks.co.uk

Balens Specialist Insurance Brokers

Tel: 01648 893 006

Email: info@balens.co.uk

www.balens.co.uk

Further Reading

Below are some books I would recommend, all of which I have very much enjoyed and have brought further understanding to different parts of my life.

Shoden: Reiki 1st Degree – *Taggart King*

Okuden: Reiki 2nd Degree – *Taggart King*

Shinpiden: Reiki Master/Teacher – *Taggart King*

Dancing with Horses (book & video) - *Klaus Ferdinand Hempfling*

The Secret – *Rhonda Byrne*

The Power of Now – *Eckhart Tolle*

The Alchemist – *Paulo Coelho*

Straight From The Horses Mouth – *Amelia Kinkade*

Learn to 'see'

Staring into the fire, the dancing flames do burn,

As we let go off seeing the physical our eyes begin to learn,

The pictures forth do come, of secrets far away,

An understanding flickers by, but shortly doth it stay,

To hold on to that moment of seeing so clearly,

The universal magic held in our hearts so dearly,

A realization of how we could be seeing,

This comes through, simply by being.

Lightning Source UK Ltd.
Milton Keynes UK
UKOW07f2022091116

287295UK00010B/437/P